Praise for Amy McLaren and
PASSION *to* PURPOSE

*"Amy's book will show you how to have a lasting impact
with the things that light you up."*

— **Russell Brunson**, *New York Times* bestselling author

*"Amy McLaren will teach you how to turn your big sky dreams into a
reality. If you have a fire inside you that longs to live a more creative,
meaningful, and passionate life, don't wait. It's never too late or early
to live like you mean it. Let this inspiring book be your roadmap."*

— **Kris Carr**, *New York Times* bestselling author

*"Leading the life you long for requires daring and intention.
Amy will show you the way."*

— **Michael Hyatt**, *New York Times* bestselling author

*"Passion to Purpose isn't just a battle cry for women with unwav-
ering certainty that they were made for more—it's a 7-step battle
plan. My dear friend Amy McLaren's heart-centered, illustrative,
and transformative roadmap will empower you to move through
self-doubt, find your inspiration, and change your life (and the world
while you're at it). Passion to Purpose is like a how-to manual from
a trusted friend. Amy's life experiences serve as a framework. She has
lived what she teaches. And what's so special about Amy's leadership
is that when you take on the challenge of finding your purpose, the
world opens up for you. Yes, your purpose can become your livelihood.
Yes, your passion can shape the life of your dreams. And yes, you can
impact the world in greater, more beautiful strokes than you've ever
imagined. No doubt about it, Passion to Purpose is your catalyst,
the perfect place to start the rest of your life."*

— **Amy Porterfield**, entrepreneur and host of *The Online
Marketing Made Easy Podcast*

*"If you want to live a passion-filled life and make a huge impact,
this book is a practical, inspiring guide that will help you get there."*

— **Kate Northrup**, entrepreneur and bestselling author of *Do Less*

T0026649

PASSION
to PURPOSE

PASSION
to PURPOSE

a seven-step journey to shed
self-doubt, find inspiration,
and change your life
(and the world)
for the better

Amy McLaren

HAY HOUSE, INC.
Carlsbad, California • New York City
London • Sydney • New Delhi

Published in the United States by: Hay House, Inc.: www.hayhouse.com® • *Published in Australia by:* Hay House Australia Pty. Ltd.: www.hayhouse.com. au • *Published in the United Kingdom by:* Hay House UK, Ltd.: www.hayhouse. co.uk • *Published in India by:* Hay House Publishers India: www.hayhouse.co.in

Cover design: Mandy Kain • *Interior design:* Nick C. Welch

Library of Congress has cataloged the earlier edition as follows:

Names: McLaren, Amy, 1980 June 17- author.
Title: Passion to purpose : a seven-step journey to shed self-doubt, find
   inspiration, and change your life (and the world) for the better / Amy
   McLaren.
Identifiers: LCCN 2021029209 | ISBN 9781401958947 (hardcover) | ISBN
   9781401958954 (ebook)
Subjects: LCSH: Self-actualization (Psychology) | Self-realization. | Goal
   (Psychology) | Career development.
Classification: LCC BF637.S4 M35 2020 | DDC 158.1--dc23
LC record available at https://lccn.loc.gov/2021029209

Tradepaper ISBN: 978-1-4019-6917-2
E-book ISBN: 978-1-4019-5895-4
Audiobook ISBN: 978-1-4019-5899-2

10 9 8 7 6 5 4 3 2 1
1st edition, August 2021
2nd edition, August 2022

SUSTAINABLE FORESTRY INITIATIVE
Certified Chain of Custody
Promoting Sustainable Forestry
www.sfiprogram.org
SFI-01268
SFI label applies to the text stock

Printed in the United States of America

For my children, Marla and Sam: May you always have the courage to see possibilities where most people see obstacles, and to live your lives with purpose and passion.

To my husband, Stu: Thank you for the light and inspiration you continue to pour into our children's lives, as well as my own. I love you.

And for any woman out there who has struggled to discover and own your passion: Let this book be a guide to bringing you back home to yourself, and to fully owning and accepting your unique contribution to the world.

CONTENTS

NOTE FROM THE AUTHOR

What if you decided that today was the day you were going to finally get back to what matters to you? What if you took five minutes out of the day to accomplish something you were passionate about? What if I told you that you could use this passion not just to further your well-being but to do more good in the world, and to make an impact that touches the hearts and lives of countless people?

Let me be clear: I'm not talking about your children's passions, or the stuff your friends, family, or spouse love to do.

I am talking about *you*, and what *you* love to do.

In fact, can you imagine if we all took a few minutes and used what we are passionate about to give back to the world and make it a better place?

As I sit here on my office floor, with a large mug of Earl Grey tea beside me, wrapped in a luxurious new blanket that I picked up in Peru just last week, I'm so grateful for the amazing places my passion has taken me.

My passion for travel has sent me zigzagging across the world doing some pretty crazy things, from riding a 50cc (a *very* small motorcycle) across the Sahara Desert in Morocco, to traveling by rickshaw more than 1,200 kilometers through India, to attending university for a year in Australia, to teaching English as a foreign language in schools across Europe and Southeast Asia, to gorilla trekking in the Congo.

Travel is a serious passion of mine, in case you haven't guessed. Over the years, I joined this passion for travel with a passion for giving back. Along with my husband, Stu, I run a multimillion-dollar global nonprofit called Village Impact, whose focus is on partnering with communities in rural Kenya to help educate every single child.

Our work is greatly centered on relationships and community, because we make more progress when we work together. I was and have always been passionate about giving back to others, and I also love working together to create change while learning from one another. Our mission as a charity is to provide access to knowledge and entrepreneurial skill-building opportunities so that the people we serve can create better futures for themselves, their families, and their communities. We started out in 2006, and to date have built 14 schools—150 classrooms. We continue to offer hope and opportunity not just to the communities who work with us in Kenya, but to the many people who've contributed to our organization and brought their passions to life in the process.

Let me tell you, passion is contagious. It has the power to ignite hearts and souls, and to light you up in such a way that you will be changed forever. Honestly, it seems like just yesterday that Stu and I had only $324 in our bank account, and I was trying to raise enough money to build our first school in Kenya (to the tune of $125,000). But when you are led by your passion, there's always a way.

I wrote *Passion to Purpose* to help you begin a journey in your life, and to turn your dream into a living, breathing reality— your purpose. What exactly do I mean by purpose? To me, your purpose is your unique contribution to the world. Everyone's purpose (and therefore, the impact they are bound to make) will have its own unique flavor. This is not really something you can quantify—it's a quality that you can feel in your heart. It is the invisible thread that connects all people and beings to a larger sense of connection and forward progress.

I know more than most people that this process of bridging your passion with your purpose takes determination, persever-ance, and grit. As a busy mom, wife, and businesswoman, my life is far from perfect, but it is filled with so many blessings that are the direct result of following my passion and being open to new opportunities, all of which have led me to where I am today. My passion for Africa and giving back has led to building a supportive global community, as well as to adopting our son, Sam, who is from South Africa (that was a grueling eight-year journey, but without our passion there to fire us up, I don't think we could have lasted that long!).

So I'm excited to show you how simply living with your passion can lead to massive opportunities, greater happiness, and a deeper sense of fulfillment and contribution.

The life I have didn't magically appear one day. I love everything I do, but I also made deliberate, and often difficult, choices to get here. My passion journey has been a long, winding one filled with tears, loss, excitement, disappointment, discovery, and opportunity. If you were to take a snapshot of my life years ago, you'd see a woman who was constantly trying to be everything to everyone—except myself. I was living in a bubble of what was considered a "normal," and conventionally successful, life. As I will share with you throughout this book, while it looked like I was happy on the outside, inside I was struggling to get back to the real me—that ever-youthful, adventurous spirit who longed to live passionately, no matter how many people told me this was impractical and impossible.

And not only did I want to live passionately, I wanted to make a massive contribution to the world. I wanted to make a real *impact*. I wanted to give back to people whose lives had thrown unimaginable hardships and difficult circumstances their way. I wanted to prove to myself and others the priceless value of kindness and generosity.

After years of difficult lessons, many of which threatened to push me into prefabricated boxes that were way too small to contain my passion, I realized that most people had it all wrong. So many of us have been taught that in order to be "good," responsible people, we must sacrifice our joy and passion and offer selfless service to the world. I've discovered that not only does this approach take its toll, but it also keeps you from making the kind of contribution that is only possible when you are bringing *more of yourself* to your life and infusing everything you do with your passion. Think about it: You can tell the difference between someone who loves what they are doing—it's abundantly clear in their entire demeanor and attitude—and someone who's only trudging along and doing it out of obligation.

Which of these is more inspiring to you? Which fills you with a greater sense of possibility and hope?

Yes, I thought so!

⌀

The benefits of turning your passion into a sense of purpose cannot be underestimated, and I share them alongside my journey from working as an unfulfilled teacher to starting Village Impact and feeling more fulfilled than I ever thought possible. In this book, I have held nothing back. I hope my story—as well as the moving accounts of business partners, donors, and the many people who have contributed to the success of Village Impact—will not only inspire you to move forward with a passion you've perhaps been sidelining for years, but will also demonstrate the positive ripple effects of allowing your passion to be the springboard for your contribution to the world.

Where there is a passion, there is always a way.

And trust me, your passion path need not entail starting a nonprofit or raising hundreds of thousands of dollars for charity. Throughout my 40-year journey, I have witnessed the difference that a simple kind gesture can make. I have seen the cumulative effects of offering a compassionate ear or supportive words to someone who could really use it.

This book is a thorough guide to living a life from a place of passionate purpose. And it's not about doing exactly the same things I did, or following a generic template, or starting a business or nonprofit. It's a guide to bringing out the *real* you and living from that place with depth every single day. For when you locate the passion that lives within, you can use it to make this world a better place. As you'll discover throughout this book, the only real guideline is to identify a genuine passion (not someone else's idea of what your life should look like). The most successful people I've ever met are the ones who understand what makes them come alive and brings them great joy—and they endeavor to spread this wealth and share it with others.

So please dispense with the "shoulds" and be very honest about what you passionately love—whether that involves talking to and understanding people from all cultures and walks of life or creating beautiful floral arrangements that turn an ordinary room into an otherworldly oasis. Seriously, nothing is ever minor or trivial in the realm of your passion.

The aim of this book is to guide you into your passion, but it is also to help you think beyond your individual self. Because when you do, your life will change. Again, as I will share throughout the coming chapters, living purposefully doesn't have to be a grand storybook adventure. It could mean giving to causes you're passionate about or creating an amazing experience for family and friends.

I'm here to tell you that what you love matters. Don't ignore your dreams, especially when it comes to how you want to leave a mark on this world. We live in turbulent times, but they are also times of great opportunity. Every single one of us is being called upon to bring our full engagement, creativity, courage, and talents to life. Joseph Campbell said, "If you follow your bliss, you put yourself on a kind of track that has been there all the while, waiting for you, and the life that you ought to be living is the one you are living. . . . Follow your bliss and don't be afraid, and doors will open where you didn't know they were going to be."

The world needs you and your passion. You were born to make an impact in the lives of your family, community, and the world—and to open doors to new, more vibrant possibilities for living and thriving on this beautiful planet. I will be with you every step of the way to show you how, and to help you turn your passion into your everyday reality and a lasting sense of purpose.

With love,
Amy McLaren

HOW THIS BOOK IS ORGANIZED

Passion to Purpose is organized into seven different parts that fold in practical tips for turning your passion into your purpose. Although the story of my journey isn't one that I offer in a completely linear way, the through line of the book is the story of Village Impact, mixed with stories and lessons from our friends, donors, and community members. Each of the following seven parts includes an introduction, mini chapters that offer "Passion Notes" with specific tips and reflection questions, as well as a conclusion.

Part I: "Open Up to Possibility" takes you, the reader, on a deep journey into your passions. The aim of this section is to reveal to you why and how following your passion is perhaps the greatest contribution you can make to humanity. I guide you through some of the challenges that I, as well as other people I know, have experienced on the journey of embracing passion, and I also offer you tangible tools for turning your passion into a natural part of your everyday life.

Part II: "Fulfill You" helps you to move through some of the obstacles that might be holding you back from truly stepping up to the plate and claiming your passion as a necessary aspect of your identity. Unfortunately, this is all too often the case for women (and men!) who delay following their passions or sacrifice the goals they want to fulfill because they view them as not enough of a priority. I offer you tips on how to prioritize your passion, especially when the day-to-day demands of life take over.

Part III: "Dream Big" is where the rubber really hits the road. This is where I share my story of funneling my passions for travel and giving back into the creation of Village Impact. I also share simple but effective ways of moving from treating your passion like a hobby you do on the side to something that has the power to change not just your life, but also other people's lives, for the better.

Part IV: "Stay the Course" moves you beyond the initial inspiration for what I call your passion project (a tangible idea for manifesting your passion in the world) to the ups and downs you might experience as you stay the course of transforming your passion into your purpose: from struggling with the need to get it "right," to maintaining motivation and momentum, to tackling any limiting beliefs you have about money and its power to help make your dreams a reality.

Part V: "Make an Impact" helps you recognize how the minor and major actions you take toward realizing your passion project can create a magnificent ripple effect that you couldn't have predicted. I also offer you advice that I learned along the way about how you can refine your goals to make an even stronger impact on the communities you aim to reach.

Speaking of which, Part VI: "Build Your Community" is all about the power of creating meaningful and lasting relationships that not only serve to support you and your passion project, but that also fuel the people in your life to contribute their passion to the world. I'll share my philosophy on what it means to build connections that reflect your highest integrity and values, and how this is different from just gathering thousands of "followers" and "fans." As my friend James Wedmore shares later in the book, it's about creating a movement!

Finally, Part VII: "Leave a Legacy" offers perspective on the long-term effects of letting your passion be a springboard for doing good in the world—and how you can use it to inspire future generations and spark even more hope and creativity in the communities you are a part of.

Ready? Let's dive in!

PART I

OPEN UP TO POSSIBILITY

I remember a time in my life when my world was blown wide open—and I realized that as much as I had already experienced, as much as I had always gravitated toward a life of travel and adventure (which my incredible parents encouraged and supported very early on), there was still a lot that I had never been exposed to.

In 2003, I had just returned home to Canada from completing my master's degree in teaching in Australia, when I decided to move to the United States with Stu. One of his first mentors, John Childers, had invited Stu to move to Fulton, Mississippi, to manage his home office. Stu declined the offer at first, as I had been away an entire year, but within minutes I was on the phone with John, and he was discussing an opportunity not just for Stu, but also for me. The perks were incredible: We got a house to live in, a car, travel to exclusive resorts, and enough money so that I was able to quickly pay off my student loans in the 18 months I was down there. It was a done deal—I mean, it even involved travel, so I was sold! But beyond the comfort that the job afforded us, I was the recipient of one of the biggest gifts of my life: the realization that there was *so much more* available to me than I had ever known.

Both Stu and I grew up in the U.K. in two wonderful, caring, and loving homes. Both his parents and mine had always encouraged us to pursue our goals and dreams, so this was no different—and yet, it was *so* different. Let me explain.

In the two-and-a half years that followed our move to Mississippi, I experienced a lot of firsts: meeting important speakers, real estate investors, and authors; having the chance to stay in a penthouse suite; and eating gourmet food, including what is now among my favorites, sushi. You've heard the cliché that the sky is the limit—but I didn't fully *get* it until I found myself immersed in a world where everyone had avoided the everyday beaten path because they preferred to off-road. And maps didn't exist for the places and experiences I was beginning to navigate. I'd always had a loving and supportive mom, dad, and brother who taught me to believe in my dreams, but suddenly I was among people who were living those dreams—people who'd clearly custom-designed their lives based on what they genuinely wanted and were deeply passionate about. What seemed "impractical" to others was totally within reach.

As it turns out, the sky wasn't the limit, after all.

When you constantly live in this mode—where you don't simply go to school, get a job, get married, have the 2.5 kids, and accumulate the predictable creature comforts—you start to open yourself up to a bigger world of possibility. You begin to think outside the boxes that were handed to you by society. And you realize that it's never too late to do what you had once only dreamed of.

The truth is, as adventure-driven as I had always been, I didn't know my limitations until meeting Stu's mentor. Simply put, you don't know what you don't know. Often our idea of the future is based on our assumptions about the way the world works and what has been taught to us; it isn't until we step into the unknown that we recognize there's far more to learn.

My parents had given me an amazing foundation, and now I was being encouraged to build on it. Of course, having my mind blown open began with following my passion for travel and being in unfamiliar situations. As a young adult learning to align with passion, I had the wonderful experience of having my world open up. I began meeting the right people. Opportunities I could never have imagined came along.

As this section will reveal, opening up to possibility is about honoring what you love to do and moving in that direction, step by step. It's about having fun with the detours instead of fearing the mistakes. It's about trusting that the path that gets created will be uniquely yours— all because you followed the bread crumbs of your passion.

Chapter 1

FOLLOW YOUR PASSION

I met Stu at Wilfrid Laurier University in Waterloo, Ontario. He was completing his honors business degree, and I was finishing my bachelors of sociology and geography. We met on one of those crazy spring-break trips. I was on a bus heading to Daytona Beach, Florida, for five days of sun, beach, and concerts. The funny thing is, I wouldn't have met Stu if my friends and I hadn't signed up for this trip at the last minute. Since we booked the trip so late, we ended up having to take a bus from Hamilton, Ontario, instead of Waterloo.

As soon as we arrived to board the bus, our eyes were distracted by a team of soccer players kicking the ball around, all wearing Wilfrid Laurier University gear. Instantly, they saw us (also decked out in our uni swag), and we connected. While on that bus crossing the American border, a U.S. Border Patrol agent came on and asked if any of us were not born in Canada—and what do you know, it was Stu and I who stood up. It turned out we were both born in the U.K. Stu moved from London when he was six, and I moved when I was ten. While I do consider Canada my home, the U.K. is very close to my heart. In some ways, it's still home to me!

As you can imagine, this shared aspect of our reality led to fast bonding. Our time in Daytona was spent hanging out with the soccer team, attending parties, and enjoying the sunshine. While we had a great time, I never got the love note that he left me on the bus on the way home. But he more than made up for it with a surprise first date, which included a treasure hunt around the town of Waterloo. He left clues under park benches (filled with rose petals) that led to his house, where he was waiting with a big smile and a bouquet of flowers. Our relationship grew from there and led to us tying the knot in 2007, seven years later.

We dated for what in other people's eyes seemed like forever. While others wondered why we waited so long to get married, for us, it was perfect. In the time we were together, we both pursued our individual passions. For him, it was his business. For me, it was traveling and volunteering around the world. He knew I was passionate about it, and I think this is what kept us together: the encouragement to pursue whatever it was that made us *us*, and me *me*.

Having this dedicated time when we didn't feel any pressure really set us up in many ways for where we are now. Because during that time of exploration, the seeds of possibility were planted. We'd given ourselves ample space and time to get a taste of all the things we liked, by ourselves and together. We both worked to make things happen. There were low points (like when we both traveled to China and I had everything stolen, including my ticket and passport) and high points (like the immense sense of gratitude I felt during the year I was working on my master's degree in primary education in Australia).

We realized early on that following our passions was medicine for everything—from cultivating deep inner joy to strong and supportive relationships.

⌒

Unfortunately, in our world today so many people have a specific idea of what following their passion looks like. That picture often involves lots of money, a life filled with peak experiences, or a high level of achievement. But passion isn't a fairy tale, nor does it involve developing superhuman abilities. It's about knowing what brings you joy—and that's absolutely attainable for anyone, starting today.

I have always defined passion as engagement with what you love, whether that's rocking a baby to sleep or speaking in front of an audience. Passion is all about that sparkly magical pixie-dust feeling that comes over us when we're truly excited about what we are doing, whatever it is. It's not limited to what we are good at; in fact I think following your passion can sometimes look like a path into the unknown. As author Marie Forleo said in a 2012 article for Oprah.com, "Passion can't be found in your head, because it lives in your heart."

In many ways, when we are connected to passion, we don't think about what we can't do, because we are so excited about the possibility of what we can do (or even what we are doing in the moment). We become so connected to what we love that we might momentarily leave behind things like fear, self-doubt, perfectionism, and all that other stuff that would normally get in our way.

Following our passion puts us into a flow state where we aren't experiencing self-consciousness or stress—even if we can only muster that for a few minutes. When we are connected to our passion, we're like little kids who are completely absorbed in whatever it is we are doing. It makes me think of my daughter and her passion for reading. When she's reading, she tunes everything out and is lost in the story, because she's doing something she truly loves. We don't need to be climbing Mount Everest or winning big awards in order to feel that way; it's available to us on a daily basis, even in the midst of seemingly boring moments.

One of the things that can get in our way, however, is the thought, "I just don't know what my passion is." The truth is, almost everyone is already connected to their passion; however, it's likely that they just don't see it as a passion, or they are somehow disconnected from it—perhaps because of habit or other obligations that have obstructed the way. I know for myself, I felt like I had my passion and then lost it again, which I will share more about later.

Even if you don't believe you know what your passion is, it's possible to discover it simply by moving toward it and taking action with your curiosity; then you'll realize that you knew it all along but probably took it for granted or didn't recognize how powerful it is.

Sometimes, if your passion isn't already obvious to you, it's just a matter of inquiring more deeply, or talking to friends and family members who know you really well. Where have they seen you shine, or light up with joy?

I also think it's a wonderful idea to connect with our early memories of passion, which tend to thread themselves into the various phases of our lives. For example, I absolutely loved organizing summer day camps for the children in my neighborhood during my early teenage years, which aligns with what I already know about my passion for creating events.

Additionally, if you are passionate about something, it's likely that you are already finding a way to incorporate it into your life. When people think of passion, they think they have to be doing it all the time every day, but this doesn't have to be the case. For example, let's say you work 9 to 5 and don't have a lot of time or energy for yourself outside of work. So what do you do on the weekends? Or your holidays? You are probably doing something you feel passionate about and that you love, even if it's sporadic or on a small scale.

This takes me to another common obstacle to connecting with passion—that is, the idea that your passion needs to be a grand mission, like writing the next great novel or solving world hunger. The truth is, it can be as simple as connecting with nature by going on a hike or sitting on a bench and admiring the view. Everyone's passion is uniquely their own. No one's passion is too big or small, and it doesn't have to look a certain way.

I often find that being curious takes us back into our passion and beyond the boundaries of "right" and "wrong." And as I've already mentioned, the mere act of leaning into an already-existing passion can open the door onto previously unthought-of possibilities. For example, I think about the lifelong friends I've made while traveling, or my love for finding unique clothing items from around the world. I'm smiling as I write this, thinking about a few amazing dresses I've found in these markets. And the fun part is, when I've worn these dresses while speaking on stages, I always get compliments—which not only make me feel good, but also remind me of the story behind the dress, how I found it, where I got it, etc. Every one of these items has a story, and these stories connect me back to my passion for travel and adventure.

Again, on some level we are *always* connected to our passions, even if it's simply an internal acknowledgement of what we love. This is why it's so critical to find a way to engage with our passions instead of simply recognizing them. This could be as easy as heading out to one of those happy-hour painting nights. It might feel like a minor step, but when we continually move toward what we love, life becomes more rewarding.

When we lean in and say yes to our lives from a place of passion, we reinforce the very best of who we are. We amplify our strengths and gifts, and we become magnets of possibility. Life starts to flow more effortlessly, and even when there are challenges, we discover resources to handle them.

It all begins with giving yourself the space to know who you are, what you want, and what lights you up. Thankfully, Stu and I have always been on the same page, even in our younger days when we started our journey of following our passion.

You might be reading this and thinking to yourself, "That's great, Amy, but that's not where I am right now. I have a lot of things and people to take care of. Who has time for exploration?" But I'm here to say that no matter how old you are or what phase of your life you're in, giving yourself the gift of exploration is a nonnegotiable if you want to live passionately and purposefully. And since you picked up this book, my guess is that's *exactly* what you're looking to do. So begin by following that nudge inside of you, even if it's only by taking baby steps.

I know that if you're reading this book, you have something inside you that you want to share with the world. For me, it's always been travel. What is it for you? Scrapbooking? Cooking?

Parenting? When you're in an exciting conversation, what are you talking about? Really think about it—what puts you in "the zone," that state of undistracted connection and enjoyment? Moreover, how can you find a way to make that a part of your life?

When I was younger, I was constantly finding ways to travel (cheaply, and I mean super cheap!). I went to Europe and got a summer job teaching English at international language schools—not because it paid well, but because it put me within a one-hour flight or a train ride to dozens of countries.

Let's say your passion is painting but it's been years since you've made anything. What baby steps can you take toward incorporating it into your life today? Now, you don't necessarily need to set up a studio in your house. But you might begin by heading to an arts-and-crafts store, buying a few basic materials, and setting aside an hour on a Sunday afternoon. Or you could invite girlfriends over for a paint party or sign up for a one-off class via Groupon.

Bottom line: You've got to listen to your deeper desires and interests and nurture the fire inside you. Don't save your dreams for a rainy day, even if it means going slow. From my experience, it's these little steps that lead to the gigantic leaps. It's these little steps that lead to clarity that might not be possible from your current vantage point. More than anything, it's these little steps that will expand the view beyond your window into an exciting world full of possibility and untold happiness.

PASSION NOTE

You don't have to get it right, you just have to get it going.

— MIKE LITMAN, SUCCESS COACH AND BESTSELLING AUTHOR OF
CONVERSATIONS WITH MILLIONAIRES

I want you to have clarity around what you truly love to do. This requires doing the work to deeply listen and then finding a way to pursue it, even if you think you don't have the time, money, or experience.

Take a moment right now and list anything and everything you've ever had an interest in. This could be passions, hobbies, or things you are merely curious about—things that have made you say, "That's fun" or "Ooh, I like that." Pay attention to what draws you in.

Maybe you loved soccer as a kid. Or had an interest in interior design back in college. Perhaps you've always wanted to learn French because you love Parisian culture, but it never felt like a practical thing to pursue. This is not the time for judgments. Just list.

Notice if there are any common themes you can identify. For example, maybe everything on your list is connected to team-work. Or a love for the arts. Or being in nature. Or interfacing with different cultures and ideas.

Now commit to taking a step this week toward one of your interests—because a passion always starts as an interest. This is the first step to acknowledging and saying yes to *you*, and leading a life of passion, purpose, and true fulfillment.

Chapter 2

GET YOUR GLOW BACK

I've learned a lot about what it means to follow my passion from my husband, Stu. Back in university, Stu studied business, and he loved everything about it: the reading, the presentations, and the creativity that was required to find solutions to people's everyday issues. In fact, I remember him doing a presentation on the push-up bra in university! Truly, he was an entrepreneur from day one. He turned down a big corporate job that he'd been recruited for, much to his parents' dismay. He didn't know exactly what he wanted, but he definitely knew that he didn't want to work for anyone.

While Stu studied his passion and began to build a business from his parents' basement, I continued to teach English overseas. The job I got teaching summer camps led to completing my master's degree in teaching. I was in love with everything I was doing. In fact, I remember lying in bed one night while teaching on a small island in Australia and thinking that life was amazing. I was excited for every day.

After our mind-blowing, two-and-a-half year experience with John, I ventured overseas by myself for a six-week, solo travel adventure, volunteering and working around South East Asia. Shortly after I returned home, Stu and I got married, and I settled into the beginning of my teaching career. For any Americans reading this book, being a teacher in Canada is extremely prestigious and lucrative compared to the U.S.

However, something was amiss for me. Over time, the luster began to drain out of my life. I felt stuck. The energy I felt while in Australia that one evening was no longer there. The light inside of me was starting to disappear. And few things in my life—including the Danielle Steel novels that kept my mind distracted or hosting parties and planning girlfriend activities—could offer that deeper fulfillment I wanted. I was simply unhappy with some aspects of my life.

I remember one evening when I was home, deflated and exhausted from a long day of teaching. It was my first year. I was fresh out of teacher's college, and I had no control over the wild kids in the grade-five class I'd been given. In fact, I was regularly disrespected. I was called a bitch nearly every day, and at one point, I even had a stapler thrown at me.

I. Had. No. Control.

It was demoralizing, to say the least.

The thing was, I couldn't quit. I *wouldn't* quit. After all, this job had afforded me some much-needed security.

Still, that night I was asking myself more questions than usual. "Is this really it? Is this what I signed up for? Is this going to be my life . . . for good? Am I really enjoying this?"

While I enjoyed the kids (at least, those who were respectful), I felt like something major was missing. This job totally lacked the "wow" factor that I had experienced in my past jobs and travel experiences. I kept reminiscing about the travel I'd done while working with John Childers, when we got to host various events in hotels around the United States. I also thought of the amazing work I'd done while directing and teaching at language schools abroad. Those positions had put fire in my soul and inspired me to wake up in the morning with so much to look forward to!

And let me tell you, when you get a glimpse of what's possible, it's hard to accept anything less. I would lie in bed each night thinking of all that Stu and I had done, seen, and achieved, and wondering, "Why did it have to stop?"

I knew in my heart that teaching wasn't my forever, but at that point, I had no idea what was. And truthfully, I felt guilty about even having these thoughts. Thousands of graduates wait years sometimes to get a full-time teaching job in Canada, and here I was, not even having supplied (substituted) for one day of my career—and I was second-guessing it?

It certainly didn't feel good. Life had once been so exciting and promising, and now I was simply following the norms that had been set out for me and doing what was expected of me: being a teacher, a wife, etc. Even worse, it felt like I was caught in a vicious cycle of just getting up, teaching, coming home, going to bed, and doing it all over again. It felt like I was stuck in a nightmarish Groundhog Day of my own making.

I knew that something had to change, but since I hadn't identified exactly what or how, I let the feelings of discontentment settle—just hoping that maybe that light inside me would shine through eventually.

Maybe this was just a phase? A quarter-life crisis, perhaps?

Maybe all I needed was to teach a different class?

Maybe I needed to be at a different school?

The answers were elusive and asking them over and over brought up so much guilt. The same thought kept creeping in: "Think about the thousands of people who would love to have this job. You should enjoy it and be grateful that you have it in the first place. You are so lucky, you didn't supply for one single day."

What I didn't realize at the time was that my questions and that creeping sense of "something isn't right" was actually a gift. Because even though I wasn't totally sure what I wanted, the first step toward getting to your yes is acknowledging your no.

As I sat in the classroom one afternoon on an unusually quiet day, I found myself daydreaming of my adventures overseas. This was not uncommon. I pretty much thought about those times 24/7. As you have probably figured out by now, I'm a nomad at heart. I love to travel, especially when it's connected to helping others. I was 23 years old and had been to more than 30 countries. I had lived with families in Thailand. I had taught and directed international language schools in Spain, England, and Taiwan. And I missed the sheer variety—the experience of always having a new day to look forward to that was nothing like the day before.

So there I was, dreaming about all the people I'd met and the places I'd been, and how I could help some of the families I had encountered on my recent travels. After all, I had witnessed just how far a dollar could go—what an impact it could have on another person's life.

That's when the light bulb went on: *This* is what ignited my spirit. *This* is what gave me that glow I'd been yearning to feel for months.

As I sat there, I thought about how much I yearned to help others, especially in some of the places I had traveled to. And someday, when I had children of my own, I wanted to show them the world. I wanted them to experience the beauty of other cultures. And I wanted them to understand the power of giving back to people—how a stranger's kindness can change lives.

I knew the source of my unhappiness. Deep inside, I wanted to have a greater impact. I wanted to help families in remote areas of the world. I wanted to continue to travel and connect with a global community. This was my passion, which I'd been living for years—and now, it was calling out to me in a bigger way.

I realized that I wanted to be back out in the world on a bigger scale than the four walls of my classroom. Now, I am not diminishing the amazing work that teachers do with their students, but I knew that this was not my mission in life. I knew, because as much as I attempted to muster excitement and gratitude for this opportunity I'd been given, I still came home day after day deflated and cranky. The worst part? It was starting to drain my relationship with my husband. Instead of enjoying quality time with each other, we spent most of it with me complaining about everything and being too exhausted to do anything. He was always supportive and encouraged me to keep thinking about those things I liked to do. He always listened and assured me that we would figure it out.

Through it all, I realized that I could relate to what a friend had said about her job being "a form of golden handcuffs holding me captive." I didn't want to be captive; I wanted to be free. I wanted to be one of those entrepreneurs Stu and I had met in Mississippi, blazing my own trail.

I was in a rut, and a big one—but one that not many people in my life fully knew the extent of. Only a few key friends, colleagues, and family members really saw how much I was not enjoying the day-to-day of teaching.

I constantly wondered, "Is the grass greener on the other side? Is my rut real? Am I imagining these things?" This cycle of ruminating and worrying only made things worse. I was angry at myself for fixating on a problem where, just maybe, there wasn't one to begin with!

I eventually ended up taking a three-year sabbatical from my job as a teacher in order to solidify what would eventually become my primary passion path: working on my charity, Village Impact (much more about that later!). And in that time, I made sure I was doing everything in my power to find the projects, activities, and other things that supported my passion and that I could say yes to wholeheartedly. Sure enough, I slowly got my glow back. But I want you to know that this didn't happen overnight. It was a process.

PASSION NOTE

There is no passion to be found playing small—in settling for a life that is less than the one you are capable of living.

— NELSON MANDELA, FORMER PRESIDENT OF SOUTH AFRICA, ANTI-APARTHEID REVOLUTIONARY, AND PHILANTHROPIST

Do you sometimes feel like your life is on a one-way track and you're not in the driver's seat? No matter how connected to passion and purpose we might be, any one of us can find ourselves in a rut. If you're in a rut like I was, the first step to regaining your glow is recognizing where you are. Offer yourself plenty of compassion in the process—but do not ignore the state of things. So often, our guilt or discomfort keeps us from fully admitting the truth to ourselves: that we are unhappy or unfulfilled, or that we wonder if something better awaits us.

I do want to offer the caveat that sometimes we think the grass is greener on the other side when the grass on our side is just fine, so I understand the reluctance that can accompany the gut stirrings that threaten to shake up our lives. It's great to be cautious, but when the sense of dissatisfaction is continuous and follows you everywhere, it's a red flag you must honor. It's a sign that there is something in your life you must examine deeply —and perhaps even say no to. Yes, this can feel like a frightening step, but it's necessary. And once you take it, you won't regret it.

I spent a significant amount of time feeling unsatisfied, and then beating myself up for feeling that way. Don't do that to yourself. At the very least, incorporate joy and passion into your life in tidbits—and over time, if you recognize that the change needs to be more dramatic (as I did), by all means, follow that internal guidance.

Take a minute or two to consider anything it's time to say no to—a toxic friendship, a job that takes more than it gives, an obligation that has been feeling too heavy of late. Remember, you don't have to take any drastic steps until you get more clarity, but clarity comes when you start saying no, even if that only looks like reclaiming a few hours of your time or releasing some of the duties and responsibilities that are weighing you down. Saying no opens up the space for an authentic and wholehearted yes. Just imagine the possibilities that come with that!

Chapter 3

FEED YOUR BRAIN

Even if you don't know how to get yourself out of a rut to regain your glow, the good news is that you don't have to know *anything*. In fact, if you feel like you're in a rut, I'm going to be the first to congratulate you. Seriously! You are at the beginning of some epic discoveries . . . as long as you are willing to do the work.

The degree to which we are willing to learn about ourselves and the world has a lot of impact on the dullness and complacency we might feel in our lives. That's why there is great power in being mindful of what you are feeding your brain on a daily basis.

As a young couple, Stu and I would go on road trips. But almost right away, we discovered we had very different preferences in regard to what we wanted to listen to in the car.

Stu would listen to self-development audio books all the time, some of his favorites being by Tony Robbins, Brian Tracy, and John C. Maxwell. That was my cue to put my headphones on and tune out to music. In those days, not so long ago, phones were not what they are today—and podcasts didn't even exist—so my options for distraction were limited.

While I loved the road trips, I didn't particularly enjoy the self-development "noise." At that time, it felt so boring to me. I remember one recording that Stu always listened to, where the man had the highest-pitched voice I had ever heard.

What's wrong with this guy? I wondered. Instead of listening to the message that Stu obviously found valuable, all I could focus on was how annoying the guy's voice was.

How had Stu and I dated for so long without me knowing that he consumed this stuff? The closer we got as a couple, the more I discovered that he was always looking for ways to improve himself. He loved using the in-between moments to learn more and better his life. Little did I know that Stu was planting seeds that would one day impact the course of my life.

With that said, my drowning out of the noise probably went on for the first few years of our relationship. The self-help and leadership books would pile up on his nightstand, while Danielle Steel and John Grisham novels piled up on mine. I enjoyed my novels because they were easy to read and were an escape from reality.

It wasn't until I read my first self-help book (after a lot of encouragement from Stu) that I started developing bigger thoughts, bigger ideas, and a bigger vision for my life. One night, I turned over in bed to see the stack of books on Stu's side. What did he get out of these boring volumes, which tended to have words like *effective, optimal, influence,* and *habits* in their titles? It seemed like each of them was just regurgitating the same ideas in a slightly different form.

Still, I was curious. So I picked one up.

At this point, I had never really read any self-development before, or thought of ways I could improve myself. I was a motivated person, but, honestly, I didn't think I had that much power to change my situation and create something new—boy was I wrong on that one. While I would often wander the aisles of the bookstore, I never really ventured into the self-help section, but one evening something inexplicably pulled me to Stu's side table of stacked books. It's crazy, because I remember that exact moment. I can recall the details of the bedroom, how many books were on the shelf, and, of course, the one I picked up to read.

The book I selected was *The Secret,* and I literally read it from cover to cover that night. Later that week, I picked up a few more books and binged on a bunch of Joe Vitale's stuff. And I have to say: I was hooked.

I think at times we have to be open to learning and changing. We can go on living the same life day after day, but until we take time to try something new or learn from someone else, we're always going to be stuck in the same spot, which will eventually become boring and unsatisfying, even if it suited us just fine at one point.

I realized that while the romances and thrillers were harmless fun, they didn't prompt me to think more deeply, to question my choices, or to consider where I might want to take my life. But Stu's little library ignited a spark within me—that part of me that longed to create, connect, and incorporate something that I was more passionate about (because teaching certainly wasn't doing it for me). More than anything, it got me asking different questions about what I really wanted in life. And truth be told, I had never really taken the time to think about it.

Simply put, these books opened me up to the possibility that I could actually do something that lit me up! And the more I read, the more I felt inspired to think and to act differently.

I was honestly surprised at how good these books were. I could see myself in the stories that the authors shared about their lives and the people they knew. It was like they were talking directly to me (self-help books have a way of doing that). Now, I'm not saying that you have to go out and read *The Secret*, but I want to encourage you to think about what you're filling your brain with. What are you reading? Who are you talking to? Are these things opening you up to possibility, or are they merely an escape or distraction? Have you ever tried picking up books that are not your "regular" reads?

The information you put into your brain has the capacity to create a healthy foundation for your passion because it gets you thinking beyond your bubble. When you feed your brain with new knowledge and information—whether it's through the books you read, websites you visit, or music you listen to—you quickly find the vision you once had for your life expanding and transforming. You find yourself seeking new sources of information that expand your mind and heart—and then you start to become a resource for other people.

In my case, Stu was one of the people who made me realize that I could customize my life rather than continue to absorb information in a habitual way (and my guess is that he learned this from all the stuff he was listening to in the car!). I've since learned that scientists have also confirmed that we can rewire the parts of our brain that determine our thoughts, emotions, and reactions. There is no better way I can think of to do that than to expose ourselves to new knowledge, which can break us out of stale patterns of thinking and behaving.

You can start the process by inquiring about the topics you connect with or feel curious about. Offer yourself time to browse the aisles of bookstores or do Google searches on unexpected topics. Let yourself go down the rabbit hole of discovery. Start following the bread crumbs. Through the joy of exploration, you'll quickly recognize that the world isn't as confined and predictable as we sometimes make it out to be.

PASSION NOTE

The real question is, what are you going to do now? What do you choose now? . . . When people start focusing on what they want, what they don't want falls away, and what they want expands, and the other part disappears.

— RHONDA BYRNE, MEDIA PRODUCER AND BESTSELLING AUTHOR OF *THE SECRET*

Here is a short list of some of the most transformative books I've read that I know you would love, too:

- **Anything by Wayne Dyer:** In my mind, Wayne Dyer is the godfather of self-help, and his beautiful books range from exercising the power of positive thinking to conscious parenting to living a spiritually enlightened life. Check out *The Power of Intention* as well as *Change Your Thoughts—Change Your Life*.

- ***Everything Is Figureoutable* by Marie Forleo:** This incredible book, written by the award-winning business coach Marie Forleo, is all about training your brain to think positively and creatively, especially when things don't go your way. It's a must-read for anyone who's allowed fear or doubt to get in the way of their passion.

- ***The One Thing* by Gary Keller and Jay Papasan:** If you've ever had difficulty setting priorities and are tired of the clutter that results in your life, read this book! The authors will guide you on how to overcome stress, maximize productivity, and get your energy back—all by figuring out that one thing that really counts in your life.

- ***Essentialism* by Greg McKeown:** Similar to *The One Thing*, this book is about shifting your focus to the stuff that's truly essential in your life and eliminating anything that isn't. It's a powerful reminder of the choices we can make to free up our time, energy, and purpose.

My challenge for you is to find one of the books on this list and put the audiobook on or pick it up and read it. Many of us who didn't love school are resistant to learning as adults, but the world is full of incredible books and information, and a lot of it is stuff we were not exposed to in school.

And while you're at it, please pay attention to whom you're surrounding yourself with, what you're listening to, and what you're watching. All of these things have an impact, even if it seems like they are just harmless entertainment. This isn't to say that the occasional Netflix binge is bad for you. My husband and I love a good marathon of bad TV. At the same time, you have to ask yourself: "Is this the norm for me? How am I spending most of my time, and on what?"

You don't have to change anything overnight, but maybe one of those hours you spend watching reruns of *Friends* can be put toward reading that book you decided to pick up. Whatever the case, just remember that nobody is perfect—we all have things it would serve us to work on and improve. Thankfully, self-improvement can be as fun as it is life-changing!

Chapter 4

KEEP MOVING FORWARD

Knowledge is power, and one of the best ways to gain self-knowledge is to continue to move forward in your life. So often, we get stuck in predictable ruts that place limits on our sense of possibility. This is why I like to look back on my life and reflect on important turning points, changes, risks I took, and even actions that felt like mistakes at the time. No matter where I ended up, I know in retrospect that all of it was progress—because it served to move me into newness and change, which are the hallmarks of possibility.

Everything that has ever happened to you is an important component of your life story, and when you stop to look at all of it, you get to see the narrative arc. You come to understand that growth is seldom the result of stability or unchanging circumstances. I mean, think about it: Everything is constantly changing, and if we can't be flexible and find ways to adjust, we usually end up jinxing ourselves, and we don't make any progress.

For me, choosing passion is directly connected to my willingness to learn about myself, and to shift my thinking and behavior when needed. When I examine my life, it hasn't always looked the way it does now; it didn't start or end with the dream job. Everything that has meaning to me is the result of my ability to keep moving forward; in this way, the path was never predetermined—it pretty much created itself along the way.

I want to take you back a little bit, because as I look back, I think there are a few simple lessons I learned along the way that can give you clarity. So let's time-travel to when I wore turtlenecks (like, every day) in the fall and winter, and didn't understand why women couldn't just wear them under sweaters. (Hello, Canadian readers: Do you remember Northern Getaway and Northern Reflections?) I was skinny, tall, and wore baggy clothing. I had little to no confidence, except on the ski hill, where I raced and spent most weekends as a teen. I was a nice, modest girl who seldom made waves, and I certainly never wanted to be in the spotlight. In essence, I was a people pleaser.

After high school, I headed to university to study sociology and geography—but not until after I applied to nine different schools for nine completely different subjects! I applied for nursing, marine biology, geography, psychology—you name it. I ended up studying sociology and geography, which fed my appetite for learning about different cultures across the world. I was definitely not clear on what I wanted to do, whom I wanted to help, or what I wanted to study. Still, despite a lack of clarity and a reluctance to stir the pot, I knew I had to do something, or at least move forward. I believe this mentality helped me get where I am today, and that every step I took became a stepping-stone for where I eventually ended up.

At university, I studied hard, met some great friends, and hustled around the clock to pay for school by working two part-time jobs. I worked at the university bookstore, as well as at Canadian Tire, the department store chain. I would regularly walk up the hill about five kilometers to get to work—in rain, snow, and heat—and when I was lucky, I got a ride home. Obviously I knew that none of this was permanent. It was simply what I was doing at the time to pay for university and future projects.

I ultimately graduated, and the next step was to get a job. I didn't know exactly what I wanted to do, but once again, I knew my path wasn't a permanent position at the bookstore or Canadian

Tire. I did have an inkling that travel was in my future, so I decided that would be my next step, which is when I moved to Australia to attend Griffith University and pursue my master's degree in primary education. I had the amazing opportunity to teach on Horn Island, off the northern coast of the continent, where I had the pleasure of working with aboriginal communities.

Yes, I could've gotten a job and stayed in one spot, but I knew that wouldn't be fulfilling—and it certainly wouldn't have expanded my horizons or shown the young, insecure girl I was that she could spread her wings and fly. At an early age, I realized that life got better each time I took a leap of faith into new possibilities. People often get hung up looking for the perfect scenario and opportunity, but I learned that they come when you make them happen.

The more I kept moving forward by taking the next reasonable (and sometimes unreasonable!) step, the closer I got to understanding, solidifying, and cultivating my mega-passion for travel. That doesn't mean that life wasn't sometimes two steps forward, one step back—but I didn't let that deter me.

⌒⊷⌒

My close friend Rebecca is one of the women in the entrepreneurial mastermind I lead. (If you don't know what a mastermind is, it's a group of people who come together and meet in person or online for a period of time. During this time, they help and support each other in their businesses and other areas of personal growth.) She's a single mom with twins, and she's been through a lot in her life, from navigating a difficult relationship to persevering in her business despite setbacks. After battling postpartum depression and anxiety, she developed a life planner for new moms, whom she was passionate about helping.

Unfortunately, her planner never got off the ground, but rather than mope about it, Rebecca kept moving forward. She eventually had an opportunity to work with a doula coach, which led her to develop a membership site for aspiring doulas. Incredibly, the material she'd previously created for new moms that went into the "failed" life planner became integrated into her membership site. She'd always wanted to have an impact on mothers, and now she was getting to do it in an indirect way—by resourcing her doula community with the valuable tools she'd developed years before. Through her passion, she's changing lives every single day.

I hear a lot of stories like Rebecca's—where, even though someone might not achieve success in their chosen venture, they eventually come full circle back to the passion that inspired it . . . and they find new ways to apply that passion to their lives. This requires an enormous amount of faith in possibility, not to mention resilience in the face of failure.

Sara Blakely, the founder and CEO of Spanx, learned from her father to redefine failure at an early age. She shared on her Instagram that when the family was at the dinner table, Blakely's dad invited her and her brother to share some way they'd failed that day. The whole purpose was to celebrate effort and to get the kids into a mind-set of learning from their mistakes. "Failure for me became not trying, versus the outcome," Blakely says. Stu and I have now implemented this at our family dinners each evening, encouraging our kids to recount and celebrate our successes *and* failures.

When we get over the need for perfection, we become inspired to use our so-called failures as springboards for inspiration and curiosity. I've found that those who are willing to fail are often the most successful people I've ever met. After all, choosing passion is about constantly moving outside your comfort zone. Putting ourselves in unfamiliar situations allows us to grow as individuals. We learn to pave paths that have not been created for us beforehand, and we take great joy (and lots of notes!) in the process.

While a little direction can be powerful and give you a general sense of where you'd like to go, you don't need to have everything figured out beforehand. It's okay to pivot and make new choices, based on your experience in the moment—just as I did when I decided I no longer wanted to teach. Sadly, lots of people get stuck—out of a sense of fear, obligation, or the desire for security.

I promise you—when you keep moving in the direction of your passion, opportunities show up. You begin to meet people who are similar to you and love to do what *you* love to do! You also get to draw upon all the experiences you've gained up to this point in your life. For example, I don't regret my 10 years of teaching, as I took everything I learned—from creating meaningful lesson plans to navigating daily conflict—and applied it to other areas of my life. I also made some lifelong friendships as a teacher that I value to this very day.

I know that the pivots can feel harder as we get deeper into our careers, but studies have shown that by the time our lives are over, we end up regretting the things we didn't do more than the things we did. So don't leave room for regrets; keep moving in the direction of your passion—even if it's tiny baby steps at first.

PASSION NOTE

You need to have faith in yourself. Be brave and take risks.
You don't have to have it all figured out to move forward.

— ROY T. BENNETT, THOUGHT LEADER AND AUTHOR OF
THE LIGHT IN THE HEART

In life, you have two choices: You can either stand still or move forward. The thing is, if you're standing still, you're not learning or progressing. Life keeps moving regardless of where you are, what you think, or which decision you make. And if you don't move with life, you end up curtailing your growth and access to possibility. Again, dramatic steps can start small and gradual—like going to night school and working your way up to a degree, starting a book club that helps you expand your current circle of friends, or carving out 30 minutes to explore a blog that grabbed your interest.

Take some time to identify 10 changes, big or small, that you've made in your life over the years. Even if these changes looked like a failure on the surface (e.g., switching your major to one you disliked, entering a business venture that didn't work out, etc.), reflect on how they were important stepping-stones in the direction of your passion—because they kept you moving.

Conclusion

Even if you don't know what your passion is, the simple act of following your curiosity and taking action is the perfect starting point. Living your passion is all about cultivating a possibility mind-set, which makes your world expand. This is the beginning of accessing your greater purpose. After all, we are here for *so much more* than surviving and paying the bills. We are here to thrive and to teach others to do the same.

One of the things I know for sure is that a passion mind-set is a possibility mind-set. Identifying and following our passion with steadfast loyalty is exactly the ingredient to make a life full of growth and adventure—as well as authenticity and self-love. Because possibility doesn't just take you out into the world, it takes you back to the very core of who you are, what you were born to do, and what is most important to you.

I've met plenty of people who are anxious about the notion of possibility. It often brings up the terror of facing too many choices—almost like being presented with a gigantic menu full of stuff that sounds really, really good. "If I choose this one, it means I can't have that one. And what if I make the wrong choice? And what if I'm missing out on something even better?" And then, suddenly, you're spinning out into a host of scenarios that leave you feeling overwhelmed and in a state of paralysis. It can feel like drinking from a firehose.

I want you to rest assured. You don't have to move to an unfamiliar place or overhaul your entire life in order to expand your sense of possibility. You don't even have to know what your passion is beforehand. Trust me when I say this: You don't need to have *anything* figured out in advance!

Opening up to possibility is a gradual, lifelong journey. In fact, for most people, leaning into massive change all at once is a recipe for disaster. Expansion is often accompanied by contraction, but if we take a slow and steady approach—which begins by honoring and acknowledging our passion—the tiny explorations can and will add up to a whole lot of magic and happiness.

Enjoyment is truly the key to opening up to possibility. Exploring what is possible in your life isn't about adding another task to your to-do list or planning your coming year in explicit detail. There is no one road to success; success and passion are subjective, meaning they will look different to everyone.

Your life is a unique masterpiece; instead of trying to get it right, let it be, and let it flow.

So many people stay in their predetermined lanes, and they aren't happy there. So starting today, honor your passion, no matter what. Treasure the awareness that there *is* value in your passion, and the way you share it with the world will be unique. Take the time to do one little thing you are passionate about, and step back and marvel at the possibilities that open up.

PART II

FULFILL YOU

You'll find a major recurring theme in this book: It all begins with you. Yes, that's right: *you.*

I truly believe you simply can't connect to your purpose until you are connected to your passion. And passion can only be a constant source of fuel when you are connected to a greater sense of peace and comfort in who you are—in other words, when you're not living someone else's version of an ideal life, but rather are living your own unique vision of who you are and following the yellow brick road to all the stuff that makes you even more of who you are.

This is why you need to be willing to outgrow the box you're living in and understand that there is so much more that is possible for you than the cookie-cutter ideals society has handed down to most of us. And once you've moved in the direction of possibility, as we talked about in Part I, you're ready for the most important thing: figuring out who you *really* are and what you *really* want. True fulfillment is about getting rid of the "I need tos" and "I shoulds" and aligning with your inner compass and what's important to you. Free of resentment. And free of all the expectations that have been heaped onto you, maybe even by you!

Let me ask you: If you were to shed all the social roles that you've taken on, all the so-called accomplishments and milestones, would you still be happy with yourself, as you are, underneath all of that?

This sense of underlying pride in who you are is so important. In fact, I believe it's essential to being able to embrace your passion. People who follow their passion have a deep belief in the integrity of their dreams, which are part of who they are at their core. When we truly love ourselves, we naturally move toward fulfillment. We don't feel the need to clutter our lives with the activities, objects, and people that we're "supposed" to; we gravitate toward what makes us light up, because we know that *this is what we are here to do*!

So why waste time?

You are here to be intentional and true to yourself and what you want. You are here to connect deeply with that aspect of you that isn't a buildup of all the layers you've put on over the years (which, by the way, should only ever be there in service to your deeper self!).

Of course, doing something as profound as following your heart and fulfilling your true self is easier said than done—but it is possible. This section will show you exactly how you can peel back the layers and shift your mind-set and life so that you are always prioritizing your core, which is where your passion lives.

Chapter 5

SHIFT YOUR THINKING

Most of us carry stories about times in our lives when things looked great on the outside but an essential ingredient was missing. I've shared a bit with you about my experience in my teaching journey, but the issue of finding deeper fulfillment is common in so many areas of our lives.

I constantly thought about fulfillment and passion prior to becoming a mother and giving birth to my daughter, Marla. Before she came along, I struggled a lot with whether I truly wanted children. Honestly, as crazy and selfish as this sounds, I didn't really want my life to change, and I was concerned that entering motherhood would just mask the fact that I wasn't fulfilled and delay my chance to discover and pursue my passions.

I knew I would never be completely fulfilled if my primary identity was "Mom." I love this role, but I vehemently believe that there is more to a woman than her role as a mother. I had seen too many brilliant and passionate women sideline their dreams when they became moms—some did it willingly, as motherhood was their biggest passion (and, if so, that's amazing); others did it grudgingly, almost as if they had to simply do what was expected of them. I was determined not to let that happen to me.

Underneath it all, I realized that there was more to this anxiety that kept bubbling up. When I got right down to it, I was scared of losing my identity, and of giving up Adventurous Amy altogether. Stu and I had countless conversations that helped me dive into these fears. Deep down I wanted to be Mom and still be Adventurous Amy.

Needless to say, I understood that becoming a mother is a huge step, and that my entire life would change. Things would be different, but this didn't mean that I had to give up all the things that made me who I was at my core. When I realized that I could still do things my way (even if they required a little more time and forethought), I stopped listening to the cautionary words I constantly heard from the people around me—things like, "You won't be able to travel like you used to. Your life is going to revolve around your baby, so you need to just accept that."

I recognized that I'd swallowed a lie that many women are faced with—the lie that the changes that follow on the heels of motherhood require that they put their passions on hold, at least until the kids are a little older. I recognized that the only antidote to the lie is—you guessed it—honoring my passion.

Motherhood didn't have to be a lesson about choosing my role as nurturer and caretaker above everything else I cared about. I didn't have to put my passions on hold at all. I had to be more mindful of taking care of myself and fulfilling my needs—all of them. When Marla was young, I made sure that I maximized the times I could do things that made me feel wonderful and connected to my passion.

I know that the dance between motherhood and fulfillment in other areas of one's life is a constant struggle for so many women, especially those of us who are driven to accomplish other goals and continue chasing the rainbow of our passion. But for me, the struggle wasn't as acute when I shifted my thinking and assumed a possibility mind-set.

The more Stu and I talked about it, the more I realized that I'd adopted a mind-set that was not mine. But I didn't have to live by it anymore. This child was entering *my* world, and I could shape it however I wanted. I could take pride in my passions and incorporate them into my life. I would simultaneously be setting a powerful example. After all, wouldn't my children benefit more from a mother who was living her best life than someone who gave up on the things that brought her joy and fulfillment?

Sadly, many of us unknowingly adopt mind-sets and beliefs that are not our own, without a better solution in sight. Many times they are passed down from our mothers, grandmothers, or other women in our lives who grew up in an era that was dramatically different from what we are living today. We are surrounded by opportunity like never before.

I am here to tell you: The best solution is always pursuing what you are truly passionate about. When you are on track with your passion, you are prompted to step into the best version of yourself. Unfortunately, many of us are not encouraged to follow our passion. This is a huge reason I encourage everyone I know to get involved with a mastermind group or some other online or, better yet, in-person group to give them a built-in community, encouragement to grow, and a safe place to share their ideas. These are also spaces in which we are brought face-to-face with our thoughts and internal dialogue, which almost always shows up as critical self-talk or limiting beliefs such as, "I could never do that"; "What would [fill in the blank with your favorite judgmental person] think?"; "I don't have what it takes to go for what I really want"; or "I should just give up."

Believe me, I've been there. And anytime I'm trying something new, I find these voices creeping back. For years when I was trying to figure out whether or not I wanted to hold on to my teacher title, I struggled with this a lot. I didn't go all the way with leaving my job until well after Stu and I started Village Impact—because, honestly, I didn't fully know if it would work out to the extent it did. In some ways, being a teacher was my fail-safe: something to fall back on just in case things didn't work out.

If you have similar fears, please don't take these negative thoughts at face value. It's very likely that they're not even fundamentally yours, but that they're beliefs that got handed down to you. It's totally possible to replace them—and you should! Because everything starts with your thinking, and I do mean *everything*. The stories that you tell yourself solidify into your beliefs about what you can and cannot do, and what you should and should not want.

For years, I used to tell myself that I'm not a good speaker because I'm not comfortable with large audiences—until I had to face the fact that *this was just a story*. It seemed convincing on the surface, but it wasn't fundamentally true. I've since spoken in front of 20,000 people to date (I would be lying if I said it doesn't still terrify me)—and while I may sometimes still shake like a leaf, I know that when I am standing in my passion, I can do just about anything, because I believe in it so much.

Our internal self-talk has the power to become a self-fulfilling prophecy. When we begin to align with what is possible, we can shift our thinking so that it ultimately serves us. For example, I began to tell myself, "Speaking gives me a chance to share my passion, help others, raise money for a good cause, and show my daughter the power of sharing your passion in front of a big audience." This little tweak began to empower me in different ways. It opened me up to a new way of thinking, and of being. And it all started with really listening to myself instead of taking what I was saying for granted.

⌒⊶

I understand that telling someone to shift their thinking can sound obvious and almost too simple. But it's more about being aware of what you are saying to yourself and being intentional about shifting it to something that will serve you, instead of limiting you and making you feel awful. We all go through challenging moments that can test our faith and strength, sometimes leading to self-doubt and internal judgments. We can give ourselves compassion and honor the season we are in. At the same time, we can ready ourselves for a shift, simply by saying, "I know something has to change." Nurturing this awareness can be enough to get you to move forward.

I know this has happened for me. When I was burned out as a teacher and began immersing myself in self-help books, after a few months of reading I began to slowly see a shift in my thinking. I started to ask myself different questions. I noticed that I no longer played the victim role of feeling sorry for myself. I began acknowledging my inner voice and taking a deeper look at myself and everything around me. More than that, I began to dream.

I know this might sound crazy, but I had never really thought about dreams and what I wanted in life, and more important, *why* I wanted it. As I read these books, I began to entertain different questions that helped me to claim my passion more fully.

"What do I really want?"

"Why am I teaching?"

"Am I teaching because it's a good thing to do?"

"Because it has good benefits and a great pension plan?"

"Because I get summers off?"

Probably all of the above.

"But what truly makes me happy?"

"Am I weaving what makes me happy into my everyday life?"

"Am I taking the time to pursue my passions?"

"What can I do a little more of in pursuit of these passions?"

"How can I find others who want similar things?"

Once again, shifting your thinking isn't just about saying affirmations to yourself, although that can be a really powerful tool. It's about noticing the limitations you've put on yourself and expanding into a possibility mind-set. One of the most effective ways to do that is to begin with self-inquiry. Ask yourself questions about your passion. These should be questions that will open up your thinking to the kind of creative, and often unexpected, answers and resources that will move you forward.

So, where are you placing a box around your life and your passion? Where are the places you have adopted other people's limiting mind-sets? More important, are you ready to break free?

PASSION NOTE

People lose their way when they lose their why.

— Michael Hyatt, *New York Times* bestselling author

What do you want? What is your passion? Why do you want it?

Leadership coach Michael Hyatt and his wife, Gail, are the ones who taught me about the power of identifying our big why. When you discover your why, it can help you create your path to feeling unstuck and to light that fire deep within you. And when you find your why, it becomes a touchstone that you can always count on when you feel yourself looping in old, unhelpful patterns and swirling thoughts.

Recently I was listening to Dean Graziosi's book *Millionaire Success Habits* (he happens to be a donor for Village Impact, by the way) and he talks about how to find your why by using a method called Seven Levels Deep, that he learned from one of his mentors. In a nutshell, you start with a question like, "What do I want to do?" and ask yourself "Why is that important?" after each response, for a total of seven times.

So, for example:

Q: What do you want to do?
A: I want to travel.

Q: Why is that important to you?
A: It's important because of the new things I get to see.

Q: Why is that important to you?
A: Because I learn about other cultures and other people.

Q: Why is that important to you?
A: It's important because I see and hear other perspectives that are not my own.

Q: Why is that important to you?
A: It makes me a better, more understanding person as a whole.

Q: Why is that important to you?
A: I want to be a great role model for my children and those around me.

Q: Why is that important to you?
A: Because I want them to grow up to be kind and generous human beings.

By the time you get to the final answer, you've discovered the why that motivates you. And believe me, knowing your why is essential if you want to shift your mind-set, especially if you are in the middle of a funk or a personal low point. In fact, you can do the exercise yourself by going to 7LevelsDeep.com. Try it out now, with your passion in mind. Thank you, Dean!

Bottom line: The best way to shift your thinking is by asking yourself questions that open up your mind to possibility. Then, use that clarity to land on your bigger why. This foundation will begin moving you forward toward a life that is centered on your passion.

Chapter 6

GET FROM STUCK TO FREE

I am fortunate to encounter plenty of incredible people in my day-to-day life, many of whom have shared with me some of the factors that hold them back from pursuing the fulfillment that they sense is out there, somewhere. As I listen to these stories, it becomes clearer and clearer to me that fulfillment always begins and ends with us, and the attitude we take toward our perceived limitations.

For example, take Alyssa, my personal trainer at the gym I go to. She's a beautiful person inside and out. We have a lot of great conversations about life, love, work, and the world around us. Every year, I do an annual ladies' adventure trip to a different part of the world. The last place we went to was Morocco, and I invited Alyssa to join us. Much to my surprise, she was hesitant. "It sounds fun," she said. "Maybe." She never did venture to Morocco with me.

Months after the trip, Alyssa and I got to chatting, and she admitted to me that she regretted saying no. As our conversation became deeper, she began talking about her dad. "I actually told him that you invited me on the trip, and he said, 'Absolutely not—you can't go! It's not safe!'" It turned out that her dad wasn't a huge fan of traveling—or of doing anything that seemed "risky" or took him out of his comfort zone—and I believe he's passed that tendency down to Alyssa.

At the end of that talk, she looked at me and said, "I didn't even realize that maybe his way of thinking was holding me back."

Ultimately it is our mind-set that determines how free we are in our lives. And choosing freedom is all about cultivating the courage to take risks and move beyond our comfort zones—all for the purpose of following our passion.

Now, it could be that international travel really wasn't Alyssa's thing, but the fact that she later came to me and said she had regrets about not taking me up on the invitation sounded like she wanted to open up to what was possible in her life. And remember, it's that sense of possibility that ignites passion. When we ignore the places where we experience excitement and possibility, we often find ourselves stuck in the same stale patterns and habits, even if they don't ultimately serve us or make us happy.

There are also other ways in which we block ourselves from the freedom that can be found when we move toward possibility and passion. For example, sometimes it may not be an outside influence that's limiting us, but more a stubbornness to be right. This brings to mind a woman in my mastermind group whose messaging around her business was unclear and confusing. A number of people made powerful suggestions for how she could convey her message more effectively, but she wouldn't budge. She wasn't getting the results she wanted, but she continued to refuse to take the amazing advice of people who were willing to help her get past her block. She reminds me that if we truly desire a life and career filled with passion and joy, we have to recognize our own internal limited beliefs and mental blocks, because if we don't we all continue to remain stuck.

We get in our own way when we stubbornly stick to the path of our one-track minds, which can quickly lead us into a pit of quicksand! And trust me, all of us need help when it comes to breaking free, which is why I recommend expanding your friendship circles to include positive, possibility-minded people; joining a mastermind or other support group; and identifying self-imposed limits that were perhaps inherited from fearful or overprotective parents.

I also think it's a great idea to pay attention to our fears. For example, Alyssa's initial fear of saying yes to my invitation ended up masking a deeper desire she wasn't ready to explore. Often, our fears can be like that—they hide a deeper longing that we've been conditioned to stay away from.

Getting from stuck to free is about confronting the fears that keep us small and alienated from our passions (and believe me, a lot of us have been conditioned to fear our passions for being "too impractical," "too much of a luxury," "something that'll take me off track and make me forget my responsibilities," or fill in the blank with your chosen excuse!). Sometimes, fear is just a desire that we have silenced.

Instead of missing out on possibilities, we can take full responsibility for our well-being and joy. This is part of what it means to give ourselves the pep talk we need to go for the gold and live without regrets.

PASSION NOTE

Fear is only temporary. Regret lasts forever.

— UNKNOWN

Getting from stuck to free requires going more deeply into your personal landscape and looking at the places where you limit yourself or cycle in patterns that don't serve you. When you have a greater sense of awareness of where you're stuck, you can begin making progress. That's why I want to encourage you to identify one place in your life where you feel stuck. Look over the following checklist and choose at least one action item to address your "stuckness."

- **Acknowledge the block—I mean, *really* acknowledge it.** For example, if you are in what feels like a dead-end job, instead of overwhelming yourself with what-if scenarios or wallowing in self-pity, simply note the truth to yourself: "This job, and the way I am relating to it, isn't working." No judgments. Just sit with that awareness.

- **Identify the places in that block where perhaps you feel you've taken the wrong approach.** This can be a tough one for people, because we don't like admitting we're wrong. But remember the lesson Sara Blakely learned from her dad: Failure can be a gift, if we are choosing to learn and grow from it. What might an alternative approach be? Feel free to mine the brilliance of trusted friends and colleagues here.

- **Note whether there is something you really want to do that you don't think you can.** Where do you think this belief came from? Is it really true? This is where I love to refer to Byron Katie's method, known as The Work—a simple process she developed of remaining alert to and questioning stressful thoughts. It's a brilliant series of four questions you can ask yourself to turn around a limiting belief. They're so simple yet so effective. Write down a specific stressful thought. Then ask yourself the following questions, taking time to answer each before you move on to the next: Is it true? Can you absolutely know that it's true? How do you react when you believe that thought? Who would you be without the thought?

- **Ask yourself whether you have unconsciously adopted a mind-set that isn't really yours,** as Alyssa likely did from her dad. What could you replace that mind-set with?

- **Determine if there's something in your life that you are trying to force,** be it a relationship or a business venture. How can you take the path of least resistance, accept what is, and move toward joy?

- **Monitor your internal self-talk for a day.** What are some of the most common things you find yourself saying? Are they helping or hurting you? For example, as I'm writing this book, I am continuously fighting my negative self-talk: "Will people get value from this? I'm not a trained psychologist, so why should anyone listen to me? Do people really want to hear my story?" None of these questions serve me. In fact, they slow me down because I start second-guessing myself—and my writing comes to a crashing halt.

- **Note whether you're doing the same thing over and over again with respect to your feeling of stuckness.** For example, do you spend a lot of energy complaining about your job? Your spouse? Habits you want to change? Places you want to go and see? If you're having a hard time identifying these on your own, ask your spouse, friends, or even your kids about what you're complaining about and doing over and over.

- **Last, but not least, reframe your thoughts.** Instead of asking, "Can I?" Ask yourself, *"How* can I make this happen? *How* can I change?"

The goal in getting unstuck is to first create an awareness of what is keeping you stuck. And specifically, we're looking to nail down the thoughts that are keeping you stuck. Once you identify these and begin to ask yourself different questions such as, "How can I?" in place of "Can I?" it becomes much easier to fix or adjust your thoughts to serve you.

Chapter 7

FILL YOUR BUCKETS

The concept of life buckets has changed my world, and I know it has the ability to change yours.

I'm not sure where I first heard the term *life buckets* (basically, separating your life into all the parts that are important to you), but I know several authors talk about different versions of this key concept, including Jonathan Fields, who refers to them as "good life buckets," and offers a lot of resources. I love the idea of putting things that are important to us into compartments, buckets, etc.

Years ago, Stu and I began to analyze our lives. Instead of allowing life to just happen to us, we looked at what *we* could make happen. We looked at what we liked to do as a couple and as individuals, and we placed these wants and needs into buckets. This helped us to clarify what was missing and how we could create more joy in our lives.

These were (and still are) my buckets:

- Giving
- Travel
- Family

- Health
- Relationships
- Me Time

And these are Stu's buckets:

- Family
- Giving
- Business

- Sports and Fitness
- Adventures
- Nature

As a family, these are our buckets:

- Experiences
- Giving
- Family Time

Here are some examples of buckets that I've seen other people identify:

- Gardening
- Spending Time in Nature
- Health
- Spirituality/Personal Development
- Writing

- Reading
- Learning
- Sports
- Cars
- Cooking

You can also break down your buckets into even smaller buckets. For example, a category like Health might contain subcategories and activities that will vary wildly from person to person, depending on how each defines it. You get to customize! Also, it's a great idea to be super-specific about the actions you'll put inside your buckets, because that means you're more likely to do them.

So, what are your buckets? Are you filling them up, or are some of them empty? This is where the passions that you have already identified need to come into play. In fact, ideally, each of your passions gets its own bucket! It can take time to identify and shift your buckets, as well as fill them. But the most important thing is recognizing your passions and the goals connected to them; then it's up to you to determine how you are going to fill your buckets.

If you're in a relationship, it's smart to come into a sense of shared passion and purpose. Stu and I have shared buckets, including Giving, that have helped us birth some of our biggest dreams together, like starting our nonprofit, Village Impact. At the same time, I always encourage people (especially women) to have their own buckets so that they don't lose their sense of individual identity and joy, especially when becoming moms. This also strengthens your relationship with your spouse or significant other, because you can be cheerleaders for each other's growth and fulfillment. For example, I encourage Stu with his sports, and he supports me 100 percent in pursuing my passion for travel. Thankfully, our shared and personal buckets don't detract from our relationship—in fact, they offer us a deep sense of enrichment, happiness, purpose, and freedom.

⟨⟩

At one point a few years ago, I realized that not all of my buckets were being filled—and waiting until the time was "right" to start filling my buckets wasn't an option. I didn't want to wait to start doing the things I loved! I already knew what my buckets were, so half the battle was over. Now I had to ask myself: How can I fill them? And with what?

I had to figure out how I could infuse my adventures and desire to help others into my everyday life. Instead of sitting around and complaining or merely dreaming about the next adventure, I had to do it.

After my self-development binge, I realized I had been doing everything that *should* be done. I had the job that so many wanted, Stu and I had a beautiful house and beautiful relationship, and we had a little toddler, our daughter Marla, running around the house. At this point, we were also in the middle of our international adoption journey, which would lead to adopting our son, Sam.

But as good as it all looked on the surface and as grateful as I was for life's gifts, I was not fulfilled in the way I wanted to be. But I was almost scared to admit it. At this point, I was still teaching, and we were trying to figure out how to work my passion into my life on a daily basis.

The constant routine of being in the staff room at school and talking to other people who were biding their time and waiting for a holiday or summer to come wasn't fulfilling. I didn't want to live my life that way, with the sense that the only thing to look forward to was days or months away. I also hated the experience of not being in control of my life and schedule, of not being able to simply take off time when I wanted to. In the initial period of building Village Impact (which I'll talk about later in the book), I was also still teaching, which meant I constantly missed out on opportunities to travel or take on speaking opportunities. I felt like I was missing out on life, and that I was on someone else's clock.

But as I would soon discover, little changes in perspective can open so many doors.

Remember, it takes a simple shift of thinking to get unstuck and to identify whatever it is you need to do to fill your buckets. Just as I knew that teaching was not my forever, your current routine doesn't have to be your forever—especially if it is not ultimately fulfilling you.

A lot of people unnecessarily allow factors like age ("I'm too old/too young to do that") or perfectionism ("I don't have the right skills to do that well") deter them. But when we bust those limitations, it becomes so much easier to fill our buckets with life's bounty.

A friend of mine went back to school in her 40s to finish her undergraduate degree. She has two kids and a husband who runs a successful business. She'd given up her career to look after the kids, but now that they were older, she felt it was time to return to her passion for studying nutrition. At first, it felt surreal to be in classrooms full of 18-year-olds. She told me that she was self-conscious about being the "old lady" in the room. However, once she got past that little hang-up, she realized that she loved the classroom setting; what's more, she brought unique wisdom and perspective to it, based on her life experiences.

It's never too late to fill your bucket. But typically, you have to empty out your existing buckets and relabel them, especially if they're filled with other people's stuff and your passions are way at the bottom! In thinking about your buckets, remember that comparison is the enemy of joy. The shoulds and have-tos will likely crop up here, which is why you have to think very deeply about what is essential to your authentic well-being, and what makes you truly come alive.

PASSION NOTE

It's not selfish to love yourself, take care of yourself, and to make your happiness a priority. It's necessary.

— MANDY HALE, BESTSELLING AUTHOR AND FOUNDER OF "THE SINGLE WOMAN" MOVEMENT

Take 10 minutes to identify three to five major life buckets that are nonnegotiables in your life. Pay attention to passions that have always been with you, as well as ones that are beginning to bud and flower. It's totally fine to change your buckets as you go through different seasons of life, but what matters to you now? It might be tempting to add mundane stuff like House Maintenance to your list, but unless that really gets you going, don't add it!

Pay attention to what lights you up, what nourishes you, what restores you to your optimal self, and what fills you up with greater energy and a sense of profound fulfillment. If you are having trouble identifying your buckets, ask loved ones when and where they have really seen you shine. And while you're at it, add some spice and fun to your relationships with spouses and family members by creating separate bucket lists that help you feel you are growing and flourishing as a unit.

One of the things I recommend is not only to identify your buckets, but to also share them with someone you are close to, someone who is going to support you and cheer you on. For me, that was Stu. In doing this, it created great discussion around where we were feeling fulfilled and where we weren't. It also generated conversations around what we could do to support each other and be intentional about weaving our individual and shared passions into our everyday life.

Take a minute right now and list your three to four buckets. Use the examples earlier in the chapter to spark your thinking if you're having a hard time. Then share them. Again, the whole reason to do this is to create more and more awareness and intention around weaving your passions into all that you do.

Chapter 8

PRIORITIZE
AND CHANGE

Okay, so now that you have your buckets figured out, you know what I'm going to say next, right? It's time to prioritize.

So many moms I know tend to have grand plans and goals that end up being sidelined in order to take care of the day-to-day stuff and their families' needs. But as you already know, we absolutely *must take care of ourselves* before we can truly want to be of service to others.

For example, one of my nonnegotiable priorities is doing an annual ladies' trip that I put on my calendar months in advance—meaning that if anything else comes up and threatens to disrupt my plans, I just point to the calendar and shake my head. Seriously, you have to protect that time!

The ladies' trip began when I invited my dear friend Erin to go to India with me. Erin was my maid of honor at my wedding. We met when I was teaching in Australia, and we hit it off instantly. Erin was a force of nature. She'd ridden her bike across Canada and had huge ambitions to change the national social studies curriculum. After getting married and having children, Erin's life shifted to being a devoted and extremely involved mom, shuttling her kids from one event to the next and being a pillar in her community. Obviously, her time was limited, so at first

Erin resisted the invitation. Of course, I knew that I would go no matter who was accompanying me, even if that meant booking a spot in a group tour. But amazingly, Erin ended up coming on the trip and even invited two of her friends. Altogether, we were four—and we had a blast exploring the subcontinent.

Since then, I've done a second trip to India, and I've also been to Panama (by myself on that occasion) and Morocco with my women friends. This past year, I took an RV across California with my mastermind women. Stepping into life's greatest adventures with other women has now become a ritual that I can never give up. It's a part of my life and passion.

All too often I see people, especially women, give up their dreams and passions—sometimes because their spouses don't approve or because they believe somebody else needs them more. This is why we have to come back to our personal responsibility to follow our bliss—because nobody else can do that for us!

Prioritizing our passions can also save our relationships, because they keep resentment from festering within us. This is why I think it's important for spouses and partners to cultivate shared and individual passions, and to encourage each other every step of the way. When people told me that my traveling days were over once I had kids, I didn't let that deter me—and for his part, Stu did a lot to make sure that I was continuing to feed my passion. In fact, we've always come up with strategies to pursue our passions, no matter what.

So how do we begin to prioritize, especially if we have a lot of other things vying for our time and attention? My number-one piece of advice is accountability. For example, I have a personal trainer who is worth every penny, because having her by my side ensures that I'll do the thing I said I would: exercise! I also encourage people to invest time, money, and energy in their passions, because this is a powerful way of putting skin in the game. Nobody likes to invest in something without the promise of a return, and your passions are no different.

It's also a great idea to look at how you are spending your time on a daily, weekly, and monthly basis. You can look at your screen time if you have an iPhone to get a reality check when it comes to where you're letting your time get eaten up. Time-tracking apps enable you to look at exactly how much time you are logging when it comes to stuff like work or even scrolling through social media, but you might also want to keep a log of your regular daily habits, from chores to phone calls. Notice that even the stray minutes can add up to hours lost on activities that don't feel all that meaningful or fulfilling. Is it possible to replace those activities with items from your buckets? And can you go one further by adding those new, fun activities to your calendar?

I also love putting sticky notes with motivational mantras and to-dos all over my house, since I tend to be a highly visual person and it helps me to have visible pop-up reminders all around that reconnect me to life's touchstones. Stu tends to like putting reminders on his phone, and we both love to map out our goals for the year (e.g., my ladies' trip) well in advance. And we also like to set aside a budget early in the year for all of these important items.

Obviously, prioritizing means that you'll have to set boundaries and be highly intentional about where and how you are spending your time. For example, the bigger our business grows, the more we recognize we have to say no to social events, certain work opportunities, and anything else that takes us away from what is important to us. In addition, we are not the kinds of parents who fill our kids' lives with a constant stream of activities. We encourage them to pick two they feel great about (Marla has horseback riding and ballet; Sam has karate and gymnastics), and we do what we can to coordinate their schedules so that we still have time for what we love. Too many parents sideline their passions, but it's healthy to give your kids a narrower focus, or to occasionally skip sitting in on one of their practices, in order to find balance and maintain a relationship with what you want as an individual!

This one is especially tricky, but you'll also have to recognize the places where you continue to marginalize your passions or delay gratification by reverting to excuses like "I'll wait to do that once the kids are older" or "Maybe someday, when I've taken care of all my other responsibilities."

When I was teaching, one of the French teachers at my school always talked about her dream of going to Paris. When I asked her why she hadn't done it yet, she explained, "I will when I retire in about nine years." I understand that timing can play an important role in prioritizing, but I always encourage people I know not to put off their dreams for too long. I look back on the gorilla trek I took in the Congo in my 20s—it was extraordinary, and also very physically challenging. Those 14-hours hiking over uneven ground, sometimes climbing up steep hills, was something that may have been harder to do later in my life. Our interests, experiences, and capacities transform as we get older, meaning that our dreams will look and feel different, and perhaps so will the things we want for ourselves. So why not take action on your passions as they arise for you in the present?

I know that there are probably a lot of things in your life that will seem to take a rightful precedence over your passions, but I urge you not to be a martyr here. I know that as a parent or a busy person working full time and balancing life's obligations, it can be hard to fit it all in. But over time, when you notice that you have filled your calendar with the stuff that is important to you, you will begin to see and feel the benefits of filling your buckets.

Remember, as I've mentioned before, you can always start small—with something as simple as investing 10 minutes a day in yourself and your passions. We all have 10 minutes in a day! Or maybe you want to consider overhauling your schedule by waking up at 5:30 in the morning to get some writing done. Experiment with modifying your day-to-day habits, but don't feel pressure to change every single aspect of your routine (which, by the way, is a recipe for disaster).

Also, you will want to be careful about not taking the items in your buckets and turning them into chores to check off a lengthy to-do list. Do whatever you can to simplify. Try to find the joy in whatever it is you're doing and honor the time you've carved out as sacred time that's just for you.

PASSION NOTE

*All of our dreams can come true, if we have
the courage to pursue them.*

— WALT DISNEY, ENTREPRENEUR, ANIMATOR,
VOICE ACTOR, AND FILM PRODUCER

A lot of the women I work with have an enormous amount on their plates, which can lead to that sinking sensation that there are not enough hours in a day. But if you really look at the way you are spending your time, I promise you'll find that isn't true. It's a matter of being more intentional with the stuff you're piling on to your schedule and being creative about incorporating it into your life in different ways.

So you might not find yourself immediately applying for a job halfway around the world, but you can find time to pursue your passions in the middle of what I like to call the in-between moments.

While many of us lead busy lives as moms, business owners, wives, and friends, I argue that you can still find time in the in-between moments of your life to follow your passions. This might look like:

- Catching up on podcasts while taking the kids to school or to gymnastics or to soccer

- Finding time for meditative moments and deep breathing during walks with the dog

- Creating moments of beauty while cooking dinner

- Working on your novel every day for 30 minutes before the kids are up in the morning

I know that it can sometimes feel difficult to find time for yet another thing if you're running on empty, but this is the kind of commitment that will not just help you fill your buckets; it'll also nourish and renew you. After all, where attention goes, energy flows. And the energy of passion is a lifeline that will reenergize you.

Whatever you do, please don't stay stuck wallowing in the idea of your passions, and not making a decision. Don't get into the habit of worrying about what *other* people will think, when instead you should be thinking about *yourself* and what makes *you* happy.

Conclusion

In Part I, I shared with you the importance of following your curiosity and taking action to cultivate the possibility mind-set, and now I'm hoping that you can see the key to living your best life can't be found beneath a pile of excuses for why you need to delay your gratification; it's in going out into the world and accessing the joy that is your birthright. Trust me, this is the best way for you to set a powerful example for your children, your family, your loved ones, and anyone else who matters to you.

Many of us, especially women, are indoctrinated with the idea that we must live up to social norms around self-sacrifice and silently say no to our own desires, because children should come first. Don't get me wrong, my kids are important, but if I don't take care of myself, I'm not going to be the best version of myself that I can be—and thus, a better mom, friend, and wife. The same is true for you!

So before you move on to Part III of the book, please take a moment to get out your calendar and carve out some dedicated me time. While you're at it, make a plan for the year ahead, including retreats, vacations, staycations, and anything else that will help you access the healing power of joy.

Do this by yourself and/or with your partner. Stu and I sit down once a year to review the upcoming year ahead. We use Michael Hyatt's Best Year Ever program and book titled *Your Best Year Ever*. In this program Micheal shares a powerful and proven system for setting and achieving goals. We've since adapted it for ourselves, but we always make it an event to check in with our priorities, and as *New York Times*–bestselling author Stephen Covey would say, "Make the main thing the main thing."

Also, a part of this experience is looking back and being thankful for what we have accomplished. So often, we get caught up in what's next, instead of also appreciating where we're at.

Typically, we book a night in a hotel, no distractions, and seriously plan and talk goals for the upcoming year. We carve out two days to do this, and we put the big rocks on the calendar first: family travel, my ladies' trip, the Mum and Dad trip (meaning just Stu and me), our charity, business, and so on. We've learned the hard way that if you don't get things on the calendar, they won't happen.

Always remember that your goals should connect back to your passion. After all, a life lived from a place of pleasure and passion is more valuable than all the riches of the world, and it can truly create the kind of ripple effects that will transform the world within and around you. Take the time to dream. It's important.

PART III

DREAM BIG

My journey of passion to purpose led to living a life that I absolutely love. It all began with reframing my thoughts, filling my buckets, and refocusing my attention on my wildest dreams.

I marvel over how much this simple practice has changed my life. Now, by no means are things perfect—because no one's life is. Stu and I still have our ups, downs, and frustrations as we grow, but I'm proud of how far we have come. I went from spending years agonizing over my job and trying to work out where and how to fit in my passions, to being lit up and excited about my direction. When you're sharing what you're passionate about, things just flow. You can feel it in your soul, and people can see it in your eyes.

I'm grateful to have taken the stage alongside such influential entrepreneurs as Brendon Burchard, Amy Porterfield, Russell Brunson, Dean Graziosi, and Jeff Walker. I've spoken on my own, too, but I have to admit, I love it when Stu and I share the stage together. Maybe the audience appreciates seeing a husband-and-wife team casually banter onstage about something we are obviously both passionate about. Plus, I feel way more comfortable onstage with Stu than by myself. But my passion continues to push me out of my comfort zone, and I am getting better at speaking solo.

Depending on the kind of event we're at, the audiences are always different; sometimes they're authors, other times entrepreneurs. Often, they are personal-development buffs looking for ways to brighten their lives. The one magical golden thread that holds it all together is that everyone we talk to has the desire to create an impact and do more good in the world, and people seem to be drawn to our story—a story not without imperfection and rocky points, but still one that is dedicated to pursuing our passions and leaving an impact.

These events tend to serve as a reminder for Stu and me that what started out as a tiny idea that literally came from watching Oprah on TV has quickly snowballed into so much more. The origin story of Village Impact, which I will describe in detail in the next two sections, was truly one of the major aha moments—the kind that could have had the shelf life of a sneeze or eye blink if we weren't ready to seize it! And yes, it's been fun. But it's also been messy (very messy at times) and, at some points, a little frustrating. However, the ripple effect has proven to be so much bigger than I could have ever imagined.

What gets me through the nervous moments onstage—because there are *so* many—is knowing that our story isn't about us, but about a moment of inspiration that encourages others to push past the self-doubt and do that thing they've been thinking about. Often at these events, people come up to us afterward and share their travel stories and enthusiastically express their desire to give back. I remember talking to a woman who told us that she, too, once had dreams of starting a nonprofit—but she'd been stopped in her tracks by self-doubt and other obstacles. "Now I realize that a challenge doesn't have to be an obstacle," she told me, tears in her eyes. "Everything you have done here inspires me to go back to that dream and finally do something about it." I've also had tears in my eyes many times after these chats, and I do as I sit and write this. When I talk to these people, determination lights me up and encourages me to keep going—to keep pursuing my passion no matter what. Speaking might make me uncomfortable, but knowing that it could change lives helps get me through.

The visions we have that are born from our passions have a power and momentum that we can't predict. And I know from experience that these visions don't have to be big in order to take off. Think about it: Even the largest enterprises started with a simple word, thought, or flash of inspiration.

I believe that our biggest dreams and best ideas come from our passion. In the next few chapters, I'll share how I was inspired, from a single TV show, to find a way to raise $14,000 in less than two weeks while being led by my big dream of giving back. Sounds crazy, right? Even as I sit and write this years later, it still feels a little surreal.

You'll also gain insight into the magic that happens when you start to dream big. This is when things begin to fall into place. But this is also when self-doubt can potentially derail you. And, as I will show you, there is a way to use those feelings to fuel your passion rather than destroy your dreams.

I want to stress that while the previous chapters urged you to incorporate your passion into your everyday life, your "big idea" is something that will stretch you out of your regular routine. So at the stage of dreaming big, you're no longer trying to find ways to maintain the status quo and do your passion on the side. You're starting to consider how you can weave your passion into your everyday life in a more significant way. I encourage you to look at the bigger picture of what's possible! Granted, this will mean stepping into roles, responsibilities, and gifts that might seem a little daunting at first, but it will be worth it.

So what have you been putting off? Secretly dreaming about in your head? Or with a friend? Are you ready to commit to it? Why not show your children, family, friends, and even strangers that you're following your dreams?

When you start to put skin in the game, your passion will take on a life of its own—the same way mine did. I promise that when you answer the call of your spirit to say yes to the adventure that awaits you, you won't regret it.

Chapter 9

RUN WITH INSPIRATION

A lot of times when I talk to people who are curious about how I went from being a globe-trotting teacher to starting a global multimillion-dollar nonprofit, they ask me, "How did you make the shift and realize it was the right time to begin?"

I think the stories we have about timing are largely myths. The Western world is caught in a crazy epidemic of busy-ness and distractions that often makes us feel like we have to wait a million years before we invest in something that gratifies us. For me, I knew it was the right time because I was *inspired*. It was something that I thought about constantly. It was something that lit me up when I spoke about it, and it still does.

There's no such thing as right timing; when you get the idea, *that's* when you need to move forward with it. Inspiration is massive energy, so running with it is critical if you want to get your idea off the ground. In the beginning of creating a dream, it's all you have.

When you're inspired to do something—whether it hits you when you're in the shower, after waking up from a vivid dream, while you're hiking on the trail, or listening to a podcast—*that's* when you should do it, or at least get those thoughts onto paper. This can occur through simple actions, but I can tell you that you're most likely to keep moving when you're already inspired. Inspiration is a lightning bolt of creative power that can spark clarity, so take it as a valuable opportunity to get going!

I also want to be the first to tell you that inspiration can arise from incredibly mundane moments, like talking to a friend or watching a TV show. This was the moment for myself in which Village Impact started to take shape. At that point I had no idea that sitting down with a bowl of popcorn and a glass of wine with my husband would lead to a multimillion-dollar charity— and now, a few years later, this book you have in your hands!

At this point, I had been steadfastly filling my buckets and living in a possibility mind-set—most of the time :)—for more than a year. Don't get me wrong, this wasn't always rainbows and unicorns. Despite all the self-help books I read, there were definitely times when I felt myself begin to slip into negativity or worrying about "what if ..." scenarios instead of focusing on the present. It happens to all of us.

But for the most part, I had begun to make this shift of watching what I was thinking and constantly trying to fill my brain with positive things while focusing and thinking about what I was passionate about. And when you're open to possibility, ideas will come to you.

It happened to me that very cold and snowy December evening while watching Oprah Winfrey's show *The Big Give*. I watched as she went into a community in the U.S. and contributed $100,000 to transform the lives of one family. In minutes, it felt like my eyes were opened. What Oprah was doing was exactly what I wanted to do. It was incredibly inspiring and opened me up to how I could have a profound impact on someone's entire world. This is what I wanted to do—I wanted to have an impact. I know it sounds simple, but it was watching this show that gave me the much-needed kick in the butt to get moving on an idea that had been circulating around for the last little while.

I wanted to do what Oprah did, but I wanted to go international, mixing my passion for travel and giving back. My travel side was coming out in full force.

Many people have asked me, "Why not stay local? There is so much need right here in your home country." But my passion has always been international relations and connecting with cultures that are very different from my own. My past travel led me off the well-trodden tourist paths and into poverty-stricken areas. Seeing just how far a dollar could go in these communities was mind-blowing. So much impact can be made with $100—heck, even $1! Mixing my love of giving with international work was the perfect recipe for feeding my passion.

While I do believe there is a need for service here at home (and I certainly try to meet that need as much as I can in my daily life in Canada through school and local community fundraisers), my heart was connected to other countries around the world after all my travels. Once again, when you are on a passion path, you must ensure that your project fulfills you, first and foremost. Don't get caught up in what you should do or what others have told you your priorities should be. This might sound selfish, but it is your passion and full engagement that will best serve the people you want to reach.

At the end of the day, I know that I make a greater impact doing international work than I would with local work. Why? Because it's my passion and it lights me up.

At this point, the idea for Village Impact was nowhere close to solidified. While I knew that the inspiration had probably been stirring beneath the surface for years—particularly in the giving-back activities I'd initiated—Stu and I had no idea what we were going to do, or exactly how we would do it. But we were inspired to do *something* to help others. From there, we had a number of conversations and brainstorming sessions and a lot of late nights discussing how we were going to do it and where we would go.

There is nothing unique about our story. Every single day, inspiration strikes millions of people in millions of different ways. The willingness to take that inspiration by the reins and run with it is what sets some of us apart. So the next time you feel truly inspired, don't shrug it off and go about your day. Acknowledge the feeling that's percolating and give it space! Most important, allow it to propel you forward—because it will, if you let it. There was a reason why you were inspired in the first place.

⌐#⌐

In Stu's online community for people who want to build membership sites for their businesses, I met a woman named Christie Hawkins. Christie is a beautiful example of how, although we might not always know where our passion will lead us, we can rest assured that simple moments of inspiration can lead us to greater and greater realizations.

Christie loves to paint, and successfully launched a business teaching local painting classes in the evenings. Although it was going well, something was off, and she couldn't quite put her finger on what it was. But she stayed with it and realized that the tension was coming from the classes being in the evenings. This was causing her to miss her daughter's volleyball games. And the more games she missed, the more tension it created.

Ultimately, Christie launched an online membership site delivering the same type of lessons she shared with others in person through video tutorials. Now she has hundreds of members and gets to do both of the things she loves: teach people to paint and spend time with her daughters.

But this is where her story gets even more fun—and inspiring. Shali Denton joined Christie's membership community, and once a month she visits the Alzheimer's Care Center to paint with the residents using Christie's online lessons. Shali sent Christie a message showing the beautiful smiles of the residents holding up the paintings they had finished following Christie's lesson. "This makes my heart so happy! I love seeing the ripple effect of what art can bring to others through this membership. I never could have seen this when I started over a year ago!" Christie shared.

And that's my point. You won't know exactly where your passion will lead you. But it won't lead you anywhere if you don't follow your inspiration. Christie followed her passion for art by starting a business teaching painting classes in her local area.

That led to her teaching the same lessons online and reaching a lot more people, which led to Shali sharing the lessons during her visits to the Alzheimer's Care Center.

This is the multiplying effect of passion—it leads to greater things than we could have possibly dreamed of.

This doesn't mean you need to start a nonprofit or charity. You don't even have to initiate a project of your own; your big idea can be as simple as joining a board of directors or getting involved in a cause that stirs your heart. Whatever you do, this idea has to be something that resonates with every aspect of who you are, especially your sense of joy and purpose (since both are intertwined). Life is about injecting these passions into the day-to-day. So let yourself get inspired, and when you feel it, go with it! It will take you to some extraordinary places.

PASSION NOTE

I can't change the direction of the wind, but I can adjust my sails to always reach my destination.

— JIMMY DEAN, ENTREPRENEUR AND MUSICIAN

Sometimes when we don't know exactly what we want to do in our lives, we attempt to force the answer. I know the feeling all too well! I am an adventurer, and for years, as I was in the midst of my deep dive into personal development, I had to learn the value of patience . . . of allowing the path to reveal itself in its own time.

Sometimes, we move prematurely in the direction of big projects that don't light us up just because we feel pressure to change the situation and to make strong decisions. While I urge you to keep moving, I also urge you to move in the direction of inspiration rather than attempting a one-size-fits-all solution. It's kind of like marriage or any serious commitment: Don't say yes to the first suitor who looks good on paper; say yes to the one who truly makes your heart sing!

Take a few minutes to write down a list of at least five times when you felt deeply inspired—when you weren't forcing anything but simply allowed the feeling to arise from your deepest knowing and passion. Note whether you acted on your inspiration. If so, what happened? If not, what will you do to move in the direction of joyful inspiration in the future?

Chapter 10

PLANT THE SEEDS

After the Oprah experience, I thought to myself, "This is it!"

I wanted to help, give, and essentially be like Oprah (I mean, who doesn't?).

However, like I mentioned, I wasn't drawn to keeping my charitable venture confined to North America; rather, I wanted to give internationally. I wanted to share and give back to those families I had encountered, and who had touched me so deeply, during my travels.

The seed was planted. This was it. We had always loved giving back and had participated in many local and community events for various charities and organizations, but this was like a bigger vision of that, and it felt so right.

Stu and I had spent the previous few years building his software company, WishList Member, which I was helping with on evenings and weekends, while I still had my teaching job during the week. In the meantime, we were saving, growing a business, and continuing to give back to family, friends, and community. But I no longer wanted to wait. I wanted to raise a significant amount of money and take it to another country so that we could have one *big impact*.

At this point, people thought we were crazy. They asked:

"What do you mean, you want to be Oprah and raise money?"

"How will you raise that much money?"

"How will you get the money there?"

We didn't know if we actually had a "good" idea. And we had no idea where to take it, or what we were capable of. But I was committed and dedicated to doing something, anything that would make a tangible difference in another country.

Our Oprah episode experience took place the second week of December. I remember looking at Stu and saying, "Let's raise money and do it this Christmas."

Christmas was the only time I could go on an adventure like this. I was still teaching, which meant I didn't have a lot of flexibility. It *had* to be Christmas. *This* Christmas. I didn't want to wait. After so many years of attempting to figure it out, I had finally received the revelation I had been waiting for! I finally knew what my life's work and service was (in truth, I think I knew all along—I just needed this external sign and flash of inspiration to wake me up). I had finally figured out what I wanted to do. I felt like I was taking my passion to the next level.

At that point, we had come to the conclusion that we would travel to help a community in El Salvador. We chose El Salvador for two reasons: The first was that we had a friend in the country, and the second was that I had identified an organization we could work with that would place us with a community there that could use our help. I told Stu I would figure out all the organizational details, while it would be his task to find the connections who would help us raise the money. He's not one to shy away from challenges, but there was definitely pressure, as we had shared the idea and people were waiting to see how much we would raise and what we would do. We literally had two weeks to raise money and create a game plan for how and where we would distribute it.

Obviously, the question of where to start was paramount.

And to be honest, we didn't know the answer.

But what we *did* have felt like enough: a powerful idea (albeit one that required some financial backing). So we looked at what and who we knew and tried to determine how we could use our resources to raise that money. We asked entrepreneurial friends of ours for some help, and together we came up with what felt like a creative approach: We decided to hold a teleseminar that would double as a fundraiser. We asked several people who are well versed in the online marketing community to share what they thought the marketing trends would be for the upcoming new year. We titled it the Prediction Call. The plan was, if we could get well known expert entrepreneurs to share their predictions with us, we could then charge people to listen and the money would go to the cause. People would pay to take part in this call, making it a win-win for everyone, as guests would get the chance to learn things to help with their business, while resting assured that the money raised was going to a worthy cause and our experts would get the chance to share their message with a new community, a win-win for all.

We made a list of what our friend Russell Brunson, founder of ClickFunnels, would call his "Dream 100." Although for us, that list was a very short Dream 12. They were all highly well-known entrepreneurs whom we approached to see if they would help us with our crazy mission. While we were blessed to be friends with some incredible entrepreneurs, there were also those on our dream list who were like Oprah in the entrepreneurial community. We didn't know if they'd say yes, but we couldn't afford not to ask.

We decided on a date, not sure if anyone would even show. But they did. We had seven amazing entrepreneurs share their expertise during our very first teleseminar. They were happy to say yes to the ask, because each and every one of them shared the same values around giving back that Stu and I did—and all the participants got to experience the joy of knowing that their money would be helping kids in El Salvador. Miraculously, we raised $14,000 with that single call.

So when it comes to running with ideas, start small. Brainstorm. Reach out to supportive networks. Everything has a way of falling into place when you step up to the plate and take consistent, decisive action. And please trust that no matter where things end up, once you have planted the seeds, they will absolutely take on a life of their own. Your job is simply to stand over them lovingly as they grow.

PASSION NOTE

What makes you different or weird—that's your strength.

— Meryl Streep, Academy Award–winning actress

An important aspect of planting seeds is recognizing your gifts and how they are instrumental in bringing your project to life.

For example, I started noticing that when it came to bringing friends and family together for various birthday parties, celebrations, or to just hang out and have fun, I was the one taking the lead role, because I *loved* organizing the details and creating a memorable experience. From the invitations to the party favors to the food and decorations, I loved it (and still do) and didn't realize that it was actually a strength until people started asking me to help them organize their parties and events.

Sometimes, something will feel easy and effortless and we think that everyone knows how to do it, but that's not true. Things that may come easy to you are hard for others. So often there are clues hidden in the everyday interactions of people asking you for help with different activities. For example, my mom gets asked a lot of questions about how to run a successful Airbnb, or we're always asking my father-in-law for his help with cooking or assembling furniture, etc.

Another example is our friend Clay, who built himself an amazing home theater. Now he gets asked questions all the time about audio, video, sound, wiring, and the electrical components that are needed to bring it all together. But when Stu and I have talked to him about this being a real strength, he discounts his expertise by saying, "Oh you can just learn it on YouTube." But this is not the point—the point is that he has a strength for being able to create an unbelievable home theater experience.

What are *your* strengths?

I know you have many, because everyone does. While lots of experts focus on the importance of expanding our competence in the places that feel like challenges, I have found that we make the best contributions when we are in sync with our strengths.

Often, especially if we are bootstrapping our way into a passion project, we are put in the position of doing everything, from paying the bills to speaking about our work at big events. But what if we gave ourselves the chance to do what we do best, and to let that be our primary role?

Gallup's CliftonStrengths assessment is an online resource that helps people recognize talents in themselves that so often go unrecognized, especially in a world that is all about trying to become more "perfect" or to fix aspects of ourselves that we do not like.

Even if you haven't identified a big passion project in your life yet, I want you to know that we plant the most effective seeds when we are willing to operate from our fundamental strengths. When you focus on roles that you love, you can turn to other people to help fill in the blanks, so to speak, by lending their passion and expertise to your project.

Take a few moments to jot down five of your strengths—places where not only do you know you shine, but where you experience enjoyment and a deeper sense of purpose. Here are some examples:

- Great organizational skills

- The ability to empathize deeply with others and make them feel heard

- The gift of throwing incredible parties that have people talking about them for years afterward

- A fantastic sense of humor

- A knack for seeing the big picture and helping to solidify the larger vision of an organization or project

Trust me when I say that you have a greater impact when you start to focus on what you love to do. You will still have plenty of challenges on the path ahead, as well as opportunities to stretch outside your comfort zone—but when you are connected to yourself and your strengths, you will plant even more potent seeds.

Chapter 11

WORK WITH SELF-DOUBT

As I mentioned already, Stu and I received an onslaught of questions when we decided to give ourselves three weeks to figure out who we would help, where, and how in the world we would raise money to do it.

As pumped as we were, self-doubt crept in.

Plenty of well-meaning people were ready to pile on. They asked us, "Why don't you just support something someone else is already doing? Wouldn't that be way easier?"

I've gotten used to these kinds of questions because I received similar responses when Stu and I adopted our son, Sam, from South Africa. People would ask, "Why don't you just have your own child? Why wait for a child from overseas? Why not adopt locally?"

But my heart was screaming exactly the opposite. I was very passionate about adopting internationally. I didn't want to take the easy route.

The charitable work that Stu and I had done made me realize that not only did I want to help other people's children in far-flung places where hearts were big and opportunity was scarce—I also wanted to embrace my passion on an even more personal level. I wanted to provide a better life for a child who deserved a shot at fulfilling his or her own dreams. I wanted to live my life in such a way that I would be constantly reminded of the monumental power of love and its capacity to connect us across oceans, continents, and varied life circumstances.

In the end, our international adoption journey took us a whopping eight years. *Eight years!* In that time, we faced plenty of challenges and a stream of well-intentioned questions from friends, family, and everyone else who cared to share their opinions with us. But if there's one thing I've learned and come to value over time, it's the power of being stubborn. Sometimes when you want something, you can't listen to what others think, and you definitely can't settle for something that isn't going to fulfill you. You have to stick to what you want. That's exactly what I did, and in the end I got what I wanted: our beautiful son, who is the perfect fit for our family. (And I have my mother to thank for that streak of stubborn independence!)

When I say that our adoption was "bumpy," I'm not kidding. There was an almost intolerable number of barriers that Stu and I faced along the way. Each time we had a setback, we felt the knife twisting further into our hearts. So you can imagine how painful it was to keep hearing things like, "Why don't you just have your own child?" No one seemed to understand, much less respect, that adoption was our first choice.

I specifically remember one night when I cried myself to sleep because we had just found out that the woman who headed our adoption agency (whom we had been working with for two years) was being charged with fraud. She had been taking money from the families who came to her and using it for extravagant vacations, home renovations, and more.

Stu and I were devastated. We had poured so much time, energy, and money into our dream of welcoming a child from Ethiopia into our family, and now we were further from that dream than ever before. The worst part was, we were among 210 families impacted by this situation. This major blow essentially meant that the two and a half years were a complete waste. It was like hitting the reset button.

After attending court about the first agency, we were thrilled to hear that Mission of Tears, an agency out of Toronto, had offered to take our file. This was huge. So we started the whole process all over again.

However, with all the added delays, we faced another challenge: my biological clock. Our plan was always to adopt first and then have our own. But with everything still up in the air, and with me now in my 30s, I started to feel a different kind of pressure. I knew that I could give up my adoption dream temporarily and give birth to a child, but I also knew it would prolong the painful process even longer. After all, an adoption agency cannot refer you as a potential adoptive parent if you become pregnant, as there is an 18-month bonding window between a parent and a newborn child. This would only serve to disrupt the bond that would need to be forged between a parent and an adopted child. So I felt stuck. I wasn't getting any younger, but I really wanted our first child to be through adoption. It was a very difficult time. There was so much uncertainty, and our lives were being put on hold as we tried to navigate these decisions.

Eventually, we moved forward with trying for our own child, and we're so incredibly grateful that it led to our daughter, Marla, being born. But what that also meant was further delays with the adoption. Eighteen months after Marla was born, to the date, we were back at the adoption office, ready to pick up where we left off.

So although our adoption journey was grueling, we continued to wait. However, at the six-year mark we decided to move on. We wanted our kids to be close in age and adopting from Ethiopia was looking more and more bleak. So we scheduled a meeting with the director of the new agency we were working with to let him know that we were no longer going to proceed with the dream of international adoption. But during that meeting, something completely unexpected happened. He convinced us to stay based on the recommendation that we switch our country to South Africa. He explained that the South African program was run extremely well, and we could be home with a child within six months.

Stu and I didn't know what to say. In fact, we both became so overwhelmed with emotion that we started to cry. Our intent coming into the office was to remove ourselves from the program. But here we were being told that we could be matched and have a child within six months. Doubt turned into hope again, and after a quick conversation in the car, Stu and I decided to change our country and move forward again. Personally, this was a very emotional time. Because although we were so excited, we also began facing a lot of questions from others about our decision. Their doubts created doubts within us, which got worse when the director's six-month time line came and went.

Six months turned into nine, nine turned into ten, and before we knew it, another full year had passed and we weren't any closer to our dream. That's when Stu and I decided once and for all that we needed to move on. We couldn't keep putting our lives on hold waiting for a phone call that might never come. That's when we scheduled another meeting with the director at Mission of Tears to let him know that we were going to give up for real this time. At this point, we were approaching eight full years of waiting. But during that meeting, the director strongly encouraged us to stay the course. He couldn't legally tell us that we had been matched yet, but he just kept saying, "I strongly recommend you don't give up."

Again, we were so conflicted. We wanted to believe that we were on the verge of getting incredible news. But were we? I was second-guessing another decision to keep going but didn't want to admit it. It felt so heavy—this one decision seemed to be the one thing that was stopping us from moving forward in so many ways.

However, Stu and I both walked out to the car again—this time, not with excitement or joy but confusion and frustration. Our hearts were heavy, and the adoption felt like it was causing more tension and stress than the dream was worth. And yet despite these setbacks, we felt like the director was trying to communicate to us that we were close. There was no spreadsheet analysis or scientific fact leading our decision. It was pure intuition. Our gut instincts were telling us that we had to keep going. So we did.

A few weeks later, I checked my e-mail after teaching a kindergarten gym class; the director of the agency was asking me to give him a call immediately. I knew that this was it. I was almost terrified to pick up the phone and call him. That recess I went straight to a good friend of mine, Julie, and said, "I think we may have been matched." As I began crying, a few other staff members came around encouraging me to call. Many of them had been a part of the adoption journey since day one.

My heart was racing, and my palms were sweaty when I picked up the phone. To my astonishment and delight, the director informed me that our long wait was over. Stu and I had been matched with a beautiful baby boy named Samkelo (Sam for short). I cried and cried some more. To be totally honest, I told the director that Stu would have to call him back. Once I heard that we had been matched, I couldn't contain my emotions. Eight years of waiting, uncertainty, challenges, and frustration were all being released with one single phone call. It was a milestone moment. Our dream had finally come true.

I immediately called Stu, who was in Nashville at the time, and shared the good news. We cried together, and I explained that he would have to call the director back to get all the details, because I didn't really hear anything other than "You have been matched with a baby boy named Samkelo."

In late January 2014, when Sam was one and Marla was three, we all Skyped together for the first time. It was Sam's first birthday and his adorable smiling face was covered in cake. A few weeks later, we were on a plane to South Africa, where we spent two months getting to know the loving, curious, outgoing, openhearted boy who would be our son. He was truly meant for us. After all, when you take the first letters of Stu, Amy, and Marla, it spells SAM.

⌒#⌒

I absolutely knew that it was important for me to remain persistent, determined, and optimistic throughout this experience. But we all have self-doubt, no matter how many companies we own, how much money we have in the bank, or how prestigious our job title is. It happens to all of us, but how we allow it to affect us makes all the difference.

I would be lying if I said that I don't still experience doubt. However, today I know I can use it as fuel for my journey. Rather than allowing it to paralyze me, I let it motivate me.

I remember getting a tattoo on the back of my neck—it reads "kuamini," which means "believe" in Swahili. Getting that tattoo hurt. It was so painful, but my friend kept saying, "Amy, you had a baby! You can do this!" But I get it because belief is the antidote to self-doubt. When we remember our own competence, we realize that we are capable of so much more than our self-doubt has convinced us we are.

If you don't feel confident about your capacity to brave whatever life throws at you (and whatever amazing things your passion wants to lead you into, no matter how many naysayers you might have), build your confidence and belief in yourself by starting small, and reminding yourself of what you have done. For example, someone who wants to run a marathon who has never done it before could start by entering a 5K, working their way up to a 10K, then a 20K, and . . . before they know it, they'll be running a full marathon!

Of course, self-confidence isn't purely an inside job. It's important to surround ourselves with people who genuinely believe in us. Yes, I've said this before and I will say it again! We need friends and mentors who reflect our greatness back to us and who will hold our highest vision with as much sacredness as we do. As the biblical saying goes, "Don't cast your pearls before swine." Not to compare the people in our lives to pigs, of course, but some of the ones we will come up against won't "get" our dreams or stand behind them. That's okay. We don't have to try to convince anyone. Our allies and supporters are already among us, and it's our job to find them.

I want to emphasize that the purpose of building confidence in ourselves isn't to do away with doubt. Everyone has doubt, which isn't a bad thing! Sometimes it can help us to clarify our goals with greater rigor and commitment. Other times, it can signal the voice of our intuition and a gut feeling that isn't about shame or judgment, but about a truth we need to pay attention to. But when doubt becomes debilitating—that is, when it keeps us cycling through indecision and festering in perfectionism or excuses for why we can't follow our passion—it's time to redirect our thoughts so that we can take meaningful action.

I know that a lot of people who've been through the trials of an international adoption (or of launching a project as ambitious as a global charity) might have compromised their dream or given it up altogether, often just as they are so close to making it happen—but I was determined. And man, when I'm determined about a project, my husband always says, "Look out."

PASSION NOTE

Faith is to believe in what you do not see; the reward for that faith is to see what you believe.

— SAINT AUGUSTINE, FOURTH-CENTURY PHILOSOPHER

Take 10 minutes to sit down and write out a list of your doubts about your passion project. No matter how big or small they are, jot them down. They might include things like:

- I don't have a big enough social circle to do the thing.

- My social media presence is underwhelming.

- I don't know the first thing about [fill in the blank].

- I'm not really a leader.

Now offer yourself the utmost compassion. You are a human being trying to do the best you can. Remember that almost every big idea you can think of started out modestly. The most extraordinary people you are likely to meet are the ones who've learned to cultivate a greater belief in themselves. This doesn't mean their doubts faded away, but rather that the voice of their dreams was ultimately stronger.

Next, I want you to take 10 minutes to respond to each doubt with at least one constructive and truthful thought that helps move you in the direction of your passion project. For example, the assertion that your social circle might not be big enough might garner the following responses:

- I will identify 10 supportive people in my circle who agree to share my passion project with 10 people in their circle.

- I don't need a huge social circle—I only need to connect with people who are just as passionate about this as I am.

- I can host a benefit at my house that brings together people in the neighborhood, including people I've never had a chance to meet or talk to.

Ideally, the things you write in this list will generate ideas about resources to cultivate and actions to take that will help dispel your doubts. (Even better if those actions excite you!) Greater clarity and confidence will arise from knowing that you absolutely have the power to respond to every potential obstacle.

Conclusion

At this point, you might have questions about what your passion project could be. Instead of stressing about it, I encourage you to go back to the inspiration list you made earlier. Also revisit the buckets you identified in Part II, as well as the passions that you know move you to your core. More likely than not, a passion project that will sustain itself over time is something you've thought about previously or entertained as a possibility, even if you didn't ultimately go all the way with it.

The amazing thing about starting your own passion project is that it makes you a better person, because it deepens your sense of commitment to that which is most important to you. And it makes you realize that you *do* have a unique contribution to make in this world, and that you are the only one who can do this. Yes, you're the only one, because there is no one else like you—you're one of a kind.

Some people I've met have difficulty identifying their passion project because they think it has to be a charitable undertaking, or that it needs to be turned into a full-time career. It doesn't; it just has to be connected to something you are passionate about and that you like doing.

Let's say your passion is bodybuilding, but it's more of an individual endeavor than something that will benefit others directly. But think of all the ways you could be helping people indirectly—by showing them what's possible, by giving them permission to love and nurture their bodies, and by inspiring them to cultivate their own definition of strength and self-care. While you might not set out to help others initially, following and building on your passion will expand the number of opportunities that present themselves—opportunities you might never have dreamed of until they come along!

At a certain point, when you are following your passion, you will see that your devotion has the ability to nourish and empower so many others. The story of individual passion always ends up being much bigger than the individual. People who make life happen by following their passion are contagious in their ability to inspire others. Allowing ourselves to go there is, in a way, a form of giving back.

Listen to your gut and heart. Have faith in yourself. In this moment, if you still feel held back by doubt and indecision, ask yourself: "How can I use this as an opportunity to expand beyond my comfort zone and challenge myself to grow?"

The willingness to grow is a prerequisite for stepping into passion and purpose. You cannot hope to live an extraordinary life unless you are willing to push the envelope and step into bigger dreams—the kind that make your heart race a little and leave your palms feeling somewhat sweaty.

Trust me, this isn't a sign that you should back off. It's a sign that something *big* is around the corner and you just have to keep moving forward.

We are worthy of the very best in our lives, and our lives are depending on us to claim this vital truth. It isn't about comparing ourselves to anyone else or judging our success against some arbitrary measuring stick. We are here to express our unique gifts and destiny in the world. We are here to dream up big ideas, and to see them as fully fleshed-out realities.

PART IV

STAY THE COURSE

I hope that by now, you are as excited about incorporating passion into your life as I am, or perhaps you've realized that you have been putting your passion in the corner for too long—and now it's your time to place it front and center and inject some amazingness back into your life.

Now that you've begun to sow the seeds of possibility, I know you're probably having all kinds of feelings about where you might be heading. Among those feelings: curiosity, motivation, and, let's be real, some fear.

I'm going to level with you—in the years during which I went back and forth with myself over whether or not I wanted to remain in teaching, I experienced a lot of fear. And even as I kept moving forward, it took me years to give up my position once and for all to focus on my charity and other passions I knew I wanted to explore. Yes, as I listened to that still, small voice within that urged me toward my dreams, I became more decisive, but it definitely was not a linear process. I still had all those sleepless nights when I asked myself, "Okay, Amy, what exactly are you doing? Are you really going to throw away security for something you can't even define?" I share more about this personal transition in this section of the book.

As I stepped into my passion, I found that my life purpose became clearer and clearer. Sure, I grappled with self-doubt and all the social pressures that accompany not being able to give people a simple description when they ask you, "So, what do you do for a living?" I had to learn to navigate other people's doubt, too, and to realize it was more about them and the extent to which they were open to possibility; it wasn't about me at all!

All of this is to say: If you want to live your life with an incredible sense of passion and purpose every single day, you're going to have to do the internal and external work to stay the course, and sometimes it's hard. So many people out there do whatever they can to avoid the nail-biting anxiety that I went through (and honestly, I totally get it).

Look, it takes work to make your life happen. But the cost of falling back on the easy and predictable path is all around us. How many people do you know who are unhappy with their work, their relationships, what they're doing in their free time—with their very existence? We certainly don't have control over everything in our lives, but when we make the consistent choice to move toward our freedom, we can't unsee the possibilities we've gotten a glimpse of.

I know that my life opened up exponentially when I began practicing my purpose—that is, allowing my passion-informed dream project to become a natural, living, breathing part of who I was, not something I dreamed about.

I have seen the wistfulness, longing, and desire in the many men and women who've shared their version of "If only . . ." with me. I've seen how deferred dreams can take their toll on a person's entire life. I've seen the ensuing sense of disappointment, and how the experience of playing small can stunt a person's potential.

That's why I'm so stoked that you're here with me now. Even if you feel doubt, even if things aren't perfect (and there's no such thing, anyway), you will gain the confidence, strength, and perspective to keep moving forward and practicing your purpose if you stay the course.

Chapter 12

FORGET PERFECTION

When you're living smack in the middle of your purpose, this isn't usually something you're doing through the rose-tinted glasses of that initial dream you envisioned.

The middle is messy. And it is definitely not perfect.

But this is where you'll find the sweet spot—in the middle of the mess. This is the realm of both unpredictability and serendipity. And the only thing you need to do is keep moving forward.

When I decided that we needed to raise the money to help a school in El Salvador, it felt like we were going in the right direction. That passionate go-getter part of me that had been buried for so long slowly started to surface. And let me tell you, it wasn't perfect. In fact, it felt like we were moving two steps forward and two steps back at times, but at least I was doing *something*.

Stu and I had racked our brains to figure out whom we could reach out to and ask to help us on this crazy mission of going to El Salvador to help a school over the Christmas holidays, which was only two weeks away! After we raised money through the Prediction Call, the next challenge was getting it to the community we'd identified that needed the help. We didn't really know how we were going to help beyond donating the proceeds. But we knew, given my teaching background, that we were going into a community that needed help with educational supplies. After all, I was still teaching full time.

We were fortunate to have input from Global Volunteer Network, which suggested that we help a remote school on top of a mountain. They gave us the contact info of a local field representative who would be our point of contact for the school.

Stu and I took out the $14,000 we'd raised (and we also relied on our debit card and checkbook) and headed to El Salvador. Once we landed, we were greeted by our friend, Jose Espana. He graciously took us into his home, where we got the chance to meet his family. He also took us on a trip to Walmart, where we purchased backpacks and supplies for the children at the school we would be visiting. It felt special and heartwarming to be directly involved with something as mundane as picking out the pencils and notebooks that the kids we'd soon be meeting would use!

I will never forget the day when the field rep that Global Volunteer Network had put us in touch with picked us up outside Jose's home. A gentleman who represented the organization arrived in a small red Honda Civic that looked like it would barely make it down the road, let alone up the mountain. There was a look of worry on Jose's face, but I didn't think too much of it. After we packed our bags and said our good-byes to Jose and his family, he made us leave our number—and he talked at length to the guy from the organization who picked us up, presumably to double-check where we were going. Naturally, all of this was happening in Spanish, so Stu and I really had no idea what they were saying! Nevertheless, we jammed everything into the man's little car, and off we went.

Stu was a little anxious. After all, he appreciates a good bed and a hot shower, and while he can rough it if he needs to (and usually seems to make fast friends with fellow entrepreneurs in the countries we find ourselves in), I am naturally drawn to the unknown. Meaning, as the car made its way down narrow dirt roads and up the steep mountain, I was in heaven. Here I was, mixing travel and adventure with my dream of giving back in a big way. Everything felt *right*, so right.

We made our way up the mountain and arrived a few hours later. Our lovely host family took us in, and we stayed with them and visited the school. The kids were so excited to have Stu and I stay in the community over the Christmas vacation, and we enjoyed connecting with them, teaching a little at the local school, and learning more about their customs.

The few days we spent in the village were interesting, to say the least. And there were some deeply memorable moments that make me giggle thinking about them years later. On our first morning, our host family set out cereal and milk. We ate it—well, at least Stu did. I couldn't handle the taste of the warm milk, and my stomach began to do flip-flops. I didn't want to offend the family, so I discreetly put the cereal down the sink. Embarrassingly enough, when we left the house that morning, there was more than rain on the pavement—there was cereal, and it was everywhere! The corn flakes that we had put down the sink were all on the road, and the chickens were going crazy.

Despite those funny culture-shock moments, those days on the mountain were filled with love and support from everyone in the community. We spent the money raised on buying a photo-copier, paint and craft supplies for the school. On our way back from that small town, we also visited two orphanages. With one single visit, we were able to pay for 45 girls to attend school for an entire year.

Although that was our first and only trip to El Salvador, it was the beginning of what would soon turn into a much bigger organization. And I was still just following what I loved to do: my passion.

It was on that flight back home that Stu turned to me with a twinkle in his eyes. He said, "I get it now. Let's do it."

Finally, he understood my "crazy" need to give back to people who lived in locations off the beaten path. In his own way, he was starting to see why I have always been drawn to the nomadic life (even when that meant showering outdoors, traveling on a night train through China, or sleeping in refugee camps).

That's when Village Impact truly began. We started. We got creative. We kept moving forward, even when things felt murky.

And honestly? Running with a big idea doesn't require perfection. In fact, I believe it's a huge mistake to wait for conditions to be perfect to start living your purpose. The reason Stu and I were able to make progress is that we didn't get caught up in all the details of the big dream and kept moving forward.

⌐⊄⊃

I know that most people, including me, can freeze up or become overwhelmed when we are faced with something big and important that we want to accomplish. But as the old saying goes, "Perfect is the enemy of good," and I have also taken that to mean that perfectionism can get in the way of spreading goodness and kindness.

When we place an emphasis on looking good or getting it right, we allow our egos to get in the way, big-time. I think back to what might have happened had Stu and I decided to wait for the perfect moment to act on the spark of inspiration that filled us that December night when we watched Oprah on TV. Perhaps if we waited until the summer, when we had more time, it would have been easier and everything would have run more smoothly.

And then, I remember the enthusiasm of every single entrepreneur friend who decided to help us. I recall the absolute joy on the children's faces in that mountain village in El Salvador. I think of the girls in the orphanages we visited. And I think about how even though it felt like we were flying by the seat of our pants, we touched the hearts and lives of so many of the people we met. They didn't care if what we were doing was perfect, or if we went through all the expected bureaucratic channels (in fact, had we done the latter, I'm sure we wouldn't have had half the impact that we did!). They simply cared that *we were there*.

Have you ever considered your relationship to perfectionism? Are there places in your life where you tend to go into overwhelm if things aren't what you consider perfect? Are you hard on yourself if you don't know the A through Z of whatever it is you are passionate about? Do you tend to dwell on things that have gone wrong in the past, and this keeps you from moving toward your dream 100 percent?

You can't change anything that has happened in the past, and it certainly doesn't serve you to wallow, so can you see the bumpy moments and giant question marks as opportunities? When you make your passions a priority, everything is an opportunity. Instead of focusing on what could go wrong, you start to do what Stu and I did: You focus on what could go *right*.

The mind is powerful, and the stories we tell ourselves become the realities we live. There were times when I noticed myself going off kilter and piling on more "What might happen if everything goes south?" scenarios, as well as worrying about things I didn't have control over. For example, years later, when we decided to take our top donors to Kenya for the first donor trip Village Impact ever did, I was terrified. The idea that something might go wrong—that people might get sick, or worse, in a foreign country—made it almost impossible for me to relax. So over time, I decided to focus on what I did have control over. How could I keep taking a step forward, even if unforeseen events threw me off guard?

You've probably already noticed that people have a tendency to get all worked up over what could go wrong. This is something that's known as the negativity bias, and it's a leftover survival method that our ancestors used to stay out of mortal danger. It's an evolutionary response hardwired into us, but unfortunately it can hold us back more often than it helps us or signals actual danger. A disastrous thought in the human brain can escalate to the point that it doesn't even matter if you've experienced said disaster or not; if the imagination can see, feel, and experience it, that's as good as living it!

But the imagination is kind of magical, because you can program it to work for you rather than against you. You can focus on how amazing the road ahead is going to be—how it's going to be filled with allies who want to help you, people who *want* you to succeed, an entire universe that's conspiring to make sure you get where you need to go.

Sound overly optimistic? Maybe, but in truth, it's just as probable as that worst-case-scenario version you might be stewing over. Because wherever and however we focus our attention and energy determines the results we're likely to get.

PASSION NOTE

Progress is more important than perfection.

—SIMON SINEK, SPEAKER AND BESTSELLING AUTHOR OF *START WITH WHY*

Take a moment to consider the fears and doubts that consume you when you think of your passion project. Things ranging from "I don't know the right people to help me succeed" to "It could end up being a horrible investment."

No matter where you are with your project, I want you to really acknowledge that so many people in the world started out in exactly your position, including myself. They didn't succeed because of superhuman abilities. They succeeded because they continued to believe in the value of their dreams, and to keep considering and imagining what could go really well.

Now take a few minutes to write down a list of at least 10 things that could go right if you stayed on the road of following your passion. I'm not asking you to create a list of wishes (although I believe wishes can come true—a topic for another book!), but of the highly possible good stuff that will come about as the result of you following your passion and not getting waylaid by temporary upsets or the need to have things look a certain way. Your list may look something like this:

- I could inspire other people in a similar position to use their voice and creativity for the better.

- I could find new opportunities and people to work with.

- I could build stronger relationships and alliances with the people in my community and industry.

- I could positively impact another person, family, or community.

- I could identify things that aren't working, so I can fix them.

- I could give someone else the courage to follow their passion.

- I could join forces with people who are doing the same and/or similar things.

- I could realize strengths that I never knew I had.

- I could become more confident and learn to weather the times when the going gets tough.

- I could be a role model for my children and show the importance of spending time doing things you love.

Certainly, it will take effort and consistency to replace your worries with potential positive outcomes and remind yourself of what could go right, but when Stu and I started doing this, things began falling into place in magical ways. That didn't mean everything we wanted ended up happening (you have to make room for surprises, because that's part of the beauty of imperfection), but that our focus eased any preemptive anxiety or need for perfection. And it helped us to keep moving—to put one foot before the next and await new adventures with racing hearts and unwavering smiles. You can do it, too!

Chapter 13

MAINTAIN MOMENTUM

Watching Oprah turn her vision into a stunning reality so many years ago obviously lit a fire in my belly that continues to this day. I knew in my heart that I had to do something—even if it wasn't (at least initially) on Oprah's level.

There were so many things we had to do in order to become an official charity. After the El Salvador trip, we went through the process of getting all our paperwork together, and a year later (also during my Christmas vacation), we went to Ghana. Our hearts had always been in Africa, and we can't always explain why. Stu and I both just seem to have a heart for the continent, so following our intuition and with the help of the volunteer organization, Ghana it was.

In between, a lot of things happened. We continued to raise money and connect with as many people as we could. We put up a website. We began the long process of waiting for our official paperwork to become a registered Canadian charity to be processed. (In fact, because we ran everything through our business, we ended up paying taxes on the donations until we were official!)

We even waffled over what to call the charity. For years we called ourselves World Teacher Aid, even though we were focused on building schools, not aiding teachers. We established a reputation on the basis of that name, but when we figured out that it didn't fit with what we were doing, we realized we had to shift gears.

In other words, the work never ended (and still doesn't), and we had to constantly think about the necessary step that would take us to the next level. In later chapters, I'll share how our mission and focus gradually shifted over time to the parts of the world and the projects where we realized Village Impact would make the most difference.

The work of continuous seed-planting begins with a few simple steps. I've always found it extremely helpful to connect with other people who are doing similar things and have undertaken the same journey that I want to embark on. When I wanted to find out about volunteering abroad, I talked to people who were already doing it, as well as organizations that specialized in placing volunteers in positions around the world. I also connected with a number of NGOs (nongovernmental organizations) that were doing inspiring charitable work in far-flung regions. Although I didn't always resonate with every aspect of what other people in similar shoes were doing, talking to them helped me to determine some of the not-so-obvious next steps I wanted to take, as well as what to be prepared for on the journey ahead.

Because it's easy to get lost in all the details, which can quickly become overwhelming, I never forget to fill up my buckets. I know that I continue to gain strength and perspective by going to Kenya two to three times a year. It is deeply gratifying to me, and while I acknowledge the importance of taking the stage or strategizing on my computer, I feel closest to my mission and vision when I have filled the biggest bucket of my passion: travel.

It's so important to remind yourself of your passion and your ultimate *why* for pursuing it. It will be your primary motivator, especially when those gremlins of doubt come creeping back into your head. Sometimes those gremlins will be in the form of other people. Like I said, Stu and I came across plenty of detractors who thought we were insane for aiming so high. Let me tell you, there is no faster way to kill your idea than to expose it to naysayers, or people who will give you their advice, even though often they have not done what you are looking to accomplish. So find your people. Have conversations about your dreams with people you love and trust, those who will encourage you to dream big and take action toward realizing those dreams.

Start now and begin to make a difference *today*. You can create momentum by breaking big ideas down into manageable, bite-size chunks. It's way too easy to get discouraged by taking on the world all at once. But remember, Rome wasn't built in a day. I also want to take this moment to remind you that the actions you take can be as teeny as putting yourself on the mailing list of a person or organization you admire or setting aside an afternoon for a strategy session with a mentor. Every action counts and leads to integrating a new piece of the puzzle. Even if you don't know where to start, let your curiosity guide you and keep it moving!

To make things easier on myself, I usually put my action steps and brainstorming sessions in my calendar. (Seriously, this is a nonnegotiable.) And I do my best to enjoy the journey of getting there. Success doesn't happen overnight, but it has always felt sweeter when I stopped to smell the roses along the way.

Bottom line: Passion is fuel. Magic and synchronicities will occur along the way, but we also have to put in the time and effort that are required of us. And while we're at it, we must remember to have fun, be creative, and imagine the possibilities ahead of us.

PASSION NOTE

There is no one giant step that does it
—it's a lot of little steps.

— PETER A. COHEN, BUSINESS EXECUTIVE

I acknowledge that it takes willpower to maintain momentum, but I can't drill this home enough: More often than not, major change comes from little steps rather than giant leaps. Stu's and my success didn't happen suddenly; we've refined our leadership skills and knowledge over months and years of following our passion. We might have started with helping a school in El Salvador, but our vision expanded so much after that.

It's important to keep that flame burning, and we do this by setting goals and tracking them (this helps us maintain momentum). Can you set some goals to help bring your vision to life?

Start with setting SMART goals, something I was introduced to by author and leadership expert Michael Hyatt. The acronym describes goals that are *specific, measurable, attainable, relevant,* and *timely,* which lots of executive coaches love to talk about. I encourage you to keep taking baby steps, but allow yourself to fold these steps into your larger vision:

- **First of all, you will want to set *specific* goals that clearly articulate what you are hoping to do.** In fact, the more specific and less vague your goal is, the more likely it will be that you identify corresponding actions that support your passion project. When setting goals, I like to ask myself: "What do I want to achieve? Why? Where? How? When? With whom?"

- **Setting a *measurable* goal means that you will walk away with concrete evidence that you've reached your goal.** This could look like raising the desired amount of money or getting your book into the hands of your dream literary agent. Having a sense of what the physical manifestation of your goal will look like helps strengthen your vision.

- **Also, note whether your goal is *attainable*.** Are you putting in the right amount of effort and time to move toward it? You can shoot for the stars, but consider what you have the wherewithal to accomplish, based on the resources available to you now.

- **Next, is your goal *relevant*?** Is it connected to skills you already have? Is it going to move your vision along, or is it tangential and unrelated?

- **Finally, be sure that the goal you set is *timely*.** Set deadlines every step of the way. Be decisive, but also be willing to be flexible and realistic. There's no need to race against time if you are in this for the long haul (which I hope you are) but creating milestones for yourself enables you to acknowledge and celebrate your progress.

Now that you know all about SMART goals, how can you take each component and come up with three goals that will move forward an inspiration-fueled *big idea* you've been putting on hold? Feel free to experiment with time here: Maybe you can set a one-month goal, a six-month goal, and a one-year goal for yourself. Be sure to break your goals down into smaller steps and put them in your calendar, the way Stu and I do. You've got this!

Chapter 14

MAKE MONEY YOUR FRIEND

Invariably, when Stu and I talk about our passions, the question of money can crop up in unexpected ways. Many times, people make justifications to themselves, such as, "Well, if I had the money that you do, I could also pursue my passion," or "I have no idea how to raise large amounts of money. The thought of getting the funds I need to follow my passion is just overwhelming!"

Getting clear about your relationship to money is key when it comes to following your passion. For Stu and me, every little step we took to filling our piggy banks counted. It started with raising pennies, speaking at local churches about our goals, selling candy, and hosting garage sales and other fundraising events. Every little bit helps, and it still does today.

While we now speak on large stages and are grateful to receive millions of dollars in donations, we still face challenges. And through it all, we've had to become very solid about our relationship with money. It has required an enormous amount of reframing on our behalf. After all, when people think about money, what comes to mind is fancy cars and luxury homes, as well as the ambition that is required to be successful. Or perhaps they think of greed, corruption, and economic inequality.

When Stu and I think of money, we think of the impact we can make for the better in people's lives. Money is an energy that passes into and out of our lives, and depending on how we use it, it can do a great deal of good. For us, money is the primary fuel for our passion of helping others. It's simple: More money, more impact.

Our evolving relationship with money coincided with our evolving vision for how we wanted to help others. And we always knew we wanted to be in Africa. In the middle of trying to figure out how to infuse this passion into our lives and grow our dream of making a big impact, we were still navigating our way through our international adoption journey with our son, Sam. At this point, we had still not been matched with a child, and although we had filled out so much paperwork, we were still waiting.

But one thing was for sure—our heart was in Africa . . . it was something that we felt. So we went back to the drawing board and asked, "Who can help us continue on this journey? Who can we help in Africa? Who do we know in Africa? What country would be best?"

This is how we came back to Global Volunteer Network, the volunteer agency and foundation we'd worked with in El Salvador. They did work all over the world and directed us to one of the largest refugee camps in Ghana. At that point, Stu and I knew that we needed more money, so we hosted yet another Prediction Call fundraiser that winter. The crazy thing was, we raised double the amount of money we had before, and we were still not a charity. I didn't know how to start a charity. I didn't know who to contact! Heck, I didn't know if I would need a lawyer, an official company, business name, or website. All I knew was that I wanted to help kids in Africa.

In later chapters, I'll share more about how our passion in Africa took hold and ultimately took us to Kenya, a country that is the main focus of Village Impact and our work. But right now, I want to drive home the point that Stu and I didn't feel completely equipped or prepared. The middle is messy, after all!

However, something really shifted for us when we made the tangible realization that money was the key to all of it.

I remember being in Kenya for the first time with Stu and watching his perception of money change right in front of me. We were standing in the middle of a field. It was cold, wet, and overcast. We were chatting with community leaders about teacher salaries. We asked how much a teacher's monthly salary was, and they replied, "It's the equivalent of $100 a month."

Stu and I looked at each other and his energy shifted because in that moment he realized something that would forever change his views about money, business, and life. At the time, his company, WishList Member (a membership software company), sold licenses for roughly $100 per license. That's when Stu put two and two together. He said, "If I sell one more license and contribute the money made from that sale to this community, I can fund the full-time salary of a teacher." But then the real lightbulb went on when he realized that he wasn't limited to selling or contributing the proceeds from just one sale. "What if I sell a whole lot more licenses and contribute them? The more money we make, the more impact we can have."

From there, our ideas about what we could do, based on the money we were generating, became bigger and bigger. We realized that our limitations were not true. And that if we reframed money from being about greed and self-interest to being about kindness and generosity, the amount of good that we could do was enormous! It was also a huge leap in Stu's entrepreneurial career. He realized that he could and should be proud of making money because of all the good that can come from it.

At that point, we recognized that our prior perspectives about money had been holding us back. Stu had unconsciously placed a cap on how much money he was "allowed" to earn. In fact, at some point, we recognized that he always hit a ceiling that put him in the same income bracket as his parents, but he never seemed to bust through that ceiling. There were all kinds of ways in which Stu was unconsciously self-sabotaging. But when the realization of the impact he could make by selling more software licenses hit him, he became unstoppable.

Many of us have similar blocks when it comes to money. I never liked asking for money because it felt slimy, like I was trying to get something out of someone else. As a teen, I had many jobs, including working at my parents' cleaning company, cleaning floors after hours, but perhaps one I disliked more than that was a job cold-calling people to sell circus tickets. I absolutely hated it!

Stu has always believed that the primary vehicle for selling is storytelling, and we've seen this ring true in our business and non-profit. When we share our passion by talking about the bumps of uncertainty in the road on the way to starting Village Impact, or the powerful epiphanies we've had (like Stu's aha moment with money), people sit up in their chairs to listen. Or when Stu and I talk about the rewards and challenges of managing a family and running a business together, people see their own conditions and dreams reflected in us. There is something about stories that is deeply humanizing. And by sharing our own with others in the most genuine ways, we recognize that we open up an energetic current in which money can flow freely, without the blockages of shame, fear, and self-sabotage.

Often, people fear that having money will change them for the worse, so they don't pursue it at all. But we know from first-hand experience that all money ever really does is amplify who we already are. For example, Rachel Miller is a woman in Stu's membership community who first came into our world as a client and customer. She has a gigantic heart, which is why she longed to contribute to Village Impact in a meaningful way, but she didn't have the funds. However, by applying the teachings of Stu's community with respect to building membership sites, Rachel has generated a lot of revenue for her business and, as a result, donated $125K to Village Impact to build an entire school in Kenya.

Rachel's story is an inspiring example of how the willingness to break through our barriers around money can coincide with the dream of helping others. Again, money is a means to an end—and when our hearts are in the right places, we can bypass many of the misconceptions that surround money and allow it to elevate our sense of purpose in the world.

```
┌─────────────────────────────────────────────┐
│                PASSION NOTE                   │
│                                               │
│   Do what you love and the money will follow. │
│   — MARSHA SINETAR, EDUCATOR AND AUTHOR       │
└─────────────────────────────────────────────┘
```

Money is a funny topic. It can make people squirm uncomfortably when it comes up in conversations. There are so many emotional triggers and feelings about money that stem from our childhood—and until we get clear about what they are, it can be hard to make money our friend. Take some time now to jot down your responses to the following questions:

1. Where do you feel blocked with respect to money? (For example, "I can't seem to make enough," "I don't know how to invest my money wisely," "I'm bad with numbers," etc.)

2. What are some of the early beliefs you formed that contributed to these blocks? (For example, your parents would say things like, "We can't afford that," or "Money doesn't grow on trees," which caused you to believe that money is a scarce resource. Perhaps you were made to feel guilty for wanting more of it.)

3. How have these beliefs about money negatively impacted your ability to step more fully into your dream?

4. What are some of the wonderful things you could do if you had a more expansive mind-set about money? (Go back to the "things that could go right" exercise from Chapter 12.)

5. What are three new beliefs that you want to put in place of the old ones? (For example, "Money frees up my energy to pursue my passion and purpose in the world," "I love making money and using it to do good in the world," "Making money opens me up to my innate creativity," etc.)

For extra credit, especially if you tend to have a tight rein on your finances, I encourage you to invest in your passion by putting your money toward something that helps you spend more time on it. For example, many years ago, Stu and I decided to hire a house manager. We were spending too much time arguing over cleaning the house and cooking unhealthy meals—it was very stressful. So, we looked at our budget, and decided to say no to some things to free us up to hire help. It was a stretch, but we knew that it would release a lot of stress, give us more quality time with our kids, and create pockets of time where I could focus on my passions. I realize it's not an expense everyone can justify, but for us it's become a part of our budget that we prioritize. You may not need to hire someone full time. But could you hire someone to clean your house once a month? Or trade off with a friend where you look after their kids one night a week and they return the favor? There are many possibilities, but my point is, getting that quality time back reduces so much stress and allows you to focus on what you love.

Chapter 15

TAKE ACTION TO FIND CLARITY

Our first attempt to make an impact in Africa unfolded in a series of realizations that helped us to redefine and clarify our path moving forward. Remember that being in the messy middle requires creativity, flexibility, and the willingness to rethink what you're doing altogether. This might sound overwhelming, but it's an incredible gift on the journey of turning passion into purpose. At first, the very concept of your passion will be surrounded by hypotheticals, but it's only in getting your hands dirty, so to speak, that you will figure out what needs to happen, or whether you have to recalibrate.

We touched down on the continent of Africa in Accra, Ghana, over Christmas vacation, since I was still teaching at this point. With the tens of thousands of dollars we raised from our second Predictions Call, we were ready to contribute what we had to one of the largest refugee camps in West Africa, the Buduburam Refugee Camp, which was home to more than 8,000, mostly Liberian, refugees at the time.

The plan was to help out at a school at the refugee camp, and to also implement a breakfast program. Of course, while we were excited to help, neither of us had set foot in a refugee camp before, and had no idea what to expect. I will never forget driving up to the camp. The streets were crowded with vendors hawking all kinds of merchandise, as well as the hustle and bustle and distinct smells you can always expect to find in a busy market. What surprised me most about the camp was the sheer creativity behind some of the residents' enterprises. The camp had everything from a person cooking and selling potatoes, to a charging station for electronics, to a simple tea shop. People's resources were limited, but they were so creative with the little they had.

Our time at the camp was filled with incredible conversations with refugees. We heard stories of loss and perseverance. Whole communities had had everything taken away from them during the turbulent times in their native country. They literally had nothing—however, they had hope for themselves and their children as they began to rebuild their lives from scratch.

We spent many days at the camp's school. While we were there, we were bombarded with the reality of the challenges that people in the community were facing: hunger, poverty, abuse, mental illness, sanitation, and so much more. It was heartbreaking, and we wanted to help. We didn't have a well-thought-out strategy before arriving; we just started giving and focusing our attention wherever we felt it needed to go, from contributing to the school's breakfast program to purchasing supplies for the school. But although we thought we were doing a good thing, we realized in hindsight that we weren't really having a meaningful impact. We were actually just putting a Band-Aid on a very large problem.

Within a week, the school's attendance went from 150 to 600 kids. Parents had decided to send their kids to school because they knew that with our breakfast program, the children would get at least one good meal a day. While this looked promising on the outside, the reality was that we didn't know our contact in Ghana well enough to establish a long, trusting, mutually beneficial relationship. Plus, we didn't have the bandwidth to move to Ghana or start a team that could work with the community on a day-to-day basis. We also recognized that there was going to be little involvement and commitment from the community—and that would mean ongoing dependency on the charity to continually finance the project after it began. Our vision had always been a partnership with the community where we would help get the projects started and we would work together to keep it going. This wasn't going to happen here and we were deeply discouraged. The momentum of the project quickly sputtered out and it was back to the drawing board.

Once again, in a perfect world we might have done a lot more preplanning than we ended up doing. But all of it, as difficult as it was, served as a valuable lesson that would ultimately shape the direction of our charity and lead to a much more intentional and fleshed-out vision. Through the ups and downs and the messy middle, we were on our way to fulfilling my passion for helping on an international scale—and doing so in a way that made the most sense. For one thing, we recognized that we needed to centralize our efforts and move in the direction of what was working. Over time, as we went from funding teachers to starting a breakfast program to addressing health care and clean water, we realized that the consequences of not having a major focus were dire.

At this time on our crazy journey of figuring out how we could continue working on our passion of giving back and doing it on an international scale, Stu and I knew that we still wanted to pursue the possibility of building schools in Africa. At this point on our passion journey we believed (and still do) that education is something that can be given and never taken away.

Eventually, as I'll share later in the book, we decided that our focus was going to be on building schools in Kenya and emphasizing the long-lasting effects of kids getting a good education, which would benefit their larger communities for years to come.

⟨#⟩

Charting your progress on the path to realizing your passions is so vital. Stu and I realized that not only did we want to put our concerted efforts toward doing one thing well rather than doing an okay job on several projects, but we also figured out that we wanted to work smarter rather than harder.

In the early days of Village Impact, we hosted big annual galas; planning them was the equivalent of planning a gigantic wedding. It didn't bother me that much because I love planning events, but at the very most we would raise about $14,000 per event. From our board's perspective, it wasn't worth the time, money, or resources we were putting in—especially when we figured out that being onstage at an entrepreneur friend's event could produce at least as much funding, with less of an effort. In fact, over time, we saw that 80 percent of the funds we raised came from a small number of donors who gave larger amounts.

Figuring out an effective fundraising model took a lot of trial and error, but thankfully it was just a matter of doubling down on what already seemed to be working for us. It also helped that our best strategy entailed Stu following his passion of speaking to large audiences, so it felt like we were killing two birds with one stone!

Overall, as our businesses and family have grown, we've had to consistently evaluate what is or isn't working. Things are constantly changing. This is a continual endeavor. We are always looking for ways to be more efficient and to spend the most time we can on our passions. That can mean dividing up events we go to so that at least one of us is with our kids. We've also brought our kids along with us from time to time, especially on occasions when we realized we'd be spending the better part of the month on the road.

In addition, we used to do an annual trip where we'd take our donors to Africa, but it ended up eating into our summers. When our friend Jim Shiels, who has a passion for helping parents build deeper relationships with their children, told us, "You only get 18 summers with each of your kids," we realized that we didn't want to miss out on that precious time. So now we do a donor trip every other year with the kids, and my operations manager, Carey, may take group trips outside of that if it makes sense for our organization. These days, the donor trips themselves tend to be larger and more elaborate, but planning an event that happens less frequently is well worth it. I love the small details.

Every single discovery we made about what worked best for our business arose not from sitting and thinking about what we wanted to do, but from taking action. Action creates clarity. So don't be afraid of making mistakes. In fact, the more mistakes you make, you'll be able to change direction that much more quickly and clarify how exactly you want to be fulfilling your passion.

PASSION NOTE

Do, or do not—there is no try.

— YODA, JEDI MASTER

Determining what is and isn't working for you takes time and attention. Some of this information will be abundantly clear on first glance, but other decisions require hindsight.

I encourage you to set up a system that enables you to track your passion over time, and to determine what is and isn't working. Every week or month, keep a log of running challenges and victories. You might want to break this up into categories, such as Finances and Profit, Teamwork and Partnerships, etc. You'll also want to bring your SMART goals in. Are you accomplishing the goals you set? If not, what is getting in the way? How can you respond to these hiccups in the most constructive way possible? What do you need to shift? With whom do you need to consult?

As Stu and I figured out with the big fundraising speaking engagements we began doing in place of the galas, it's a good idea to identify where you can have the greatest impact with the least amount of effort. Try to connect opportunities for efficiency with your passion and the places you really shine, just as Stu did with his speaking events. Based on what's working in your favor and what you love to do, how can you spend more of your time and energy on those things?

Conclusion

I have talked a lot in this book about the importance of cultivating a *possibility* mind-set in order to locate and follow your passion. To turn passion into purpose, it's vital to adopt an *adventure* mind-set that allows you to step into bolder risks and unknown territory, even when your heart is going pitter-patter and you have no idea what's around the corner! Believe me, getting ready for anything that comes your way with gusto and eagerness is some of the best fuel I can think of for living a purposeful, fully engaged life.

Obviously, as I've mentioned, we are always in danger of self-sabotage on this journey, which is why we need to be vigilant about marking our internal and external growth and celebrating our wins. Getting a nonprofit off the ground—even though it's connected to our greatest passions—is hard work. That's why you need to have practical measures in place that keep you focused and persevering. In our case, we were constantly looking for ways to trim the fat and juggle our home and professional lives. We had a lot of hard conversations that helped us to clarify our goals and also keep our dream not just at the top of our minds, but in full motion out in the world.

Remember, even if it seems overwhelming, all it takes is consistent action to keep your dream alive in any way you can. Start somewhere and allow the momentum of your dream and vision to take you to the next steps. Allow yourself to be okay with not undertaking a massive amount of work all at once; instead, break your purpose into short-term and long-term goals—and recognize that it's perfectly fine to expand or modify your vision over time. If anything, tweaking your vision isn't a sign of failure—it's a sign that you are successfully evolving alongside your passion, which has a life and direction of its own!

Overall, your enthusiasm and confidence must trump skepticism, discouragement, and limiting beliefs—and you have to keep moving forward, while keeping tabs on all the progress you've made. Dan Sullivan of Strategic Coach, a business coaching program for entrepreneurs, talks a lot about the gap between where you are and where you want to be, and he always suggests charting your progress by looking back on where you were and comparing it to where you are now, which can give you the much-needed confidence to tackle bigger and bigger things.

Also, you might go through periods when it feels like nothing is working out. No matter what you do, please don't give up! Offer yourself permission to walk away for a while so you can clear the cobwebs and return to your passion with a renewed sense of purpose. Every journey, no matter how blissful and purposeful, comes with its fair share of difficulty. I know from firsthand experience that the moments when we are ready to throw in the towel can often come right before incredible breakthroughs. I encourage you to hang in there, to celebrate even the seemingly minor milestones, and allow yourself to gain strength and motivation from them in the murkier moments.

PART V

MAKE AN IMPACT

Impact is a strong and powerful word. And anyone can make an impact, no matter how young or old they are.

We make an impact daily through the thoughts we entertain, the words we speak, and the actions we take. The great news is it doesn't take years to make an impact—it can be made in seconds. Yes, that's right. In seconds, you can change someone's life. The ripple effects of the right words or right actions at the right time spread far and wide.

For me, the best way to make an impact is opening my heart and seeing what genuine kindness and generosity can do. They have the power to heal old wounds, open up previously unseen doors, and send people on paths that allow them to be rays of light and hope for their loved ones and communities. The actions you can take to make an impact can be as massive as building schools in Kenya or as seemingly minute as opening a door for a stranger and asking how their day is going. Whatever you do, remember that it all adds up. Acts of genuine kindness cost you nothing.

Naturally, everything you've been doing to live your passion purposefully is bound to make an impact, and you will continue to do so. I believe that you can be more intentional and purposeful about the impact you make by following some of the guidelines I offer in this section of the book.

Here, I'll talk about both mini-impacts, or simple but powerful acts of kindness that can generate change and hope in individual lives, as well as long-term impacts, which will fuel your passion and purpose with the sustainability that is required to create meaningful and long-lasting change. Of course, both types of impacts are equally important, and I want you to see how you can weave them into your life seamlessly.

As you read the next few chapters, I encourage you to think about the impact you'd like to make. What does that feel and look like? How will your actions serve to better the lives and futures of the communities you wish to reach? What will be the daily mini-impacts you make? What about the ones you can make as a couple, family, or group? How will you hone your long-term strategy to create a domino effect of goodness and change for the better—a legacy that will live on long after you are gone?

Maybe you want people to feel a sense of home and comfort with the food you cook, or perhaps you wish to instill self-esteem and courage in young women across the world. Remember, your dreams matter, and they totally factor in here. Whatever fuels you and fills you with joy and excitement, keep moving toward it! In fact, I encourage you to fill your life with even more of your passion; use it as a catalyst for going deeper into the communities you want to impact.

Chapter 16

CHAMPION OTHERS

Taking a stand for someone else is about the most powerful thing I can think of doing. I love rooting others on so they can continue to shine and make their own impact. To be sure, this can be simultaneously simple and profound. It can mean sticking up for someone on the playground or offering words of encouragement that help a person fulfill their true purpose. I love interviews with prominent people who share their personal stories of how their lives changed after someone, like an aunt or teacher, helped them cultivate their potential through a kind gesture or some wise advice. For it is this nurturing attention that helps people recognize and follow their passion, which leads them to make a difference in their own unique way and pay it forward by championing others.

When Stu and I were in Ghana, we met someone very special who helped us realize how little it takes to make a huge impact on someone's life. Although that trip to Ghana didn't ultimately work out, a huge part of Village Impact's origin story revolves around a special young boy we met on our journey, who continues to play a big role in our charity to this day. His name is King William.

After Stu and I left the refugee camp, where we'd been quickly overwhelmed by all the initiatives we'd started that had proven unsustainable in the long-term (from setting up a school to administering a breakfast program), we set off on an adventure to visit several remote villages that were in need of help within their schools. Before I go any further, it's important to put into context what traveling to these remote areas looked like. Essentially, there were three modes of travel to choose from: First, you could take a private taxi (which was fast, but very expensive). Second, you could travel by bus (which, although cheaper, was extremely slow and would require being in the vehicle all day to get to the villages we wanted to visit). Finally, you could opt for the *trotro*. Picture a passenger van stuffed full of people; much like a bus, it stops at several locations. The only difference is that it was a lot faster than a bus. You can flag one down if it's not full by waving a hand at the driver or conductor, who then lets you know through elaborate hand signals the direction the car is heading in.

So there Stu and I were, sitting in the very back row, squished together between five other sweaty people. It wasn't glamorous, but it did the job. After a long day of village-hopping and meeting with a variety of communities, we were nearly back to our hotel—and we were absolutely exhausted. We looked forward to grabbing a bite to eat and going to sleep. But before we got there, something happened; all of a sudden, someone screamed.

Stu and I already knew how aggressive *trotro* drivers could be, but we'd somehow gotten used to the swerving. Actually, it's more like we both just tried not to pay attention to the road ahead, because, quite frankly, there were so many times we thought we were going to hit someone or something that it was more anxiety-inducing to look. Our solution was to close our eyes or just look at each other and talk about the day.

That's exactly what we were doing when everyone in front of us started screaming. Just then, we looked up and saw a body hit the windshield of our vehicle and fly over the top of the van.

Stu and I were completely silent. We were in total shock.

"Was that a body that hit the windshield?!" I asked in a panic.

My mind immediately started racing. People were hysterically trying to get out of the van, but the driver was yelling at everyone, commanding them to stay inside. That's when the tragedy erupted into a dangerous situation for everyone. Chaos quickly ensued. Large groups of people outside clumped around the van, banged on the doors, and started demanding that the driver get out. I was terrified.

In that moment, I said to Stu, "We've got to get out—now!"

I turned around, thinking that perhaps we could jump over the back seat and exit through the rear doors. As Stu turned around, he immediately shook his head and said, "No."

I could tell by his pale, drawn face that there was a reason he'd said it, but he didn't elaborate. He said to me, "Let's get out the side doors."

What he didn't tell me at the time was that the body of the man we had hit was right behind the van. Honestly, I don't know what I would have done had I seen it, as my body was already reacting strongly to everything around us. I was beginning to feel claustrophobic and on the verge of an anxiety attack. I needed to get out of the van and drink in some fresh air. I wanted to get away from everyone and get back to our hotel so that I could feel safe and settled.

Finally, the side door opened and we quickly got out. Still in shock, I was gasping for air. My body was shaking like a leaf. Unfortunately, this didn't offer the relief I had expected. In fact, things only got worse.

The crowd had grown much bigger in the meantime. Some people had surrounded the body in a circle of protection, because cars were continuing to whiz by, seemingly unfazed by this horrific event. Then, a large man single-handedly stopped oncoming traffic and pulled a driver out of a taxi. The man began yelling at the taxi driver to take the body to the nearest hospital. Then he picked up the man who had been lying in a pool of blood behind the van and carefully placed him in the back seat of the taxi. Almost immediately afterward, he ran to our van looking for our driver. He pushed the mob aside, opened the door, and dragged the driver out. Then he opened the passenger door of the taxi that held the body and pushed our driver in.

The door slammed and the taxi took off. Although the *trotro* driver and the injured (or possibly dead) man were now gone, people were furious. They wanted our driver to pay a price for what he'd done. In the confusion and turmoil, people began to push and shove one another. Stu and I ran up the street desperately looking for someone to get us away from this scene. Just then, we saw a taxi coming toward us. We stopped the car and jumped in. I couldn't get any words out other than, "Drive . . . please drive."

As we headed back to the hotel, Stu and I barely exchanged a word. Neither of us had ever experienced anything like that before, and it had shaken us deeply. As the shock started to fade somewhat, the realization of what had happened started to hit home. Both of us began to cry. What we had witnessed had been devastating enough, but given that every member of a family is vital to its survival, we hated to think where this tragedy could lead. It was possible that this man was the primary breadwinner in his family. Not knowing if he had survived was heartbreaking, because not only did it mean a life had been lost in a brutal and avoidable accident—it also meant there would be negative ripple effects in the lives of his loved ones.

We were a mess.

Then the taxi came to a stop. We were back at our hotel. As we went inside to drop our stuff off, all we wanted to do was crawl into bed and try to forget everything that had happened. The problem was, we hadn't eaten all day, and we had an early morning flight. We had to grab something, because it would likely be our last meal before getting to the airport and onto our transcontinental flight.

We quickly changed clothes and headed out the door to find a restaurant. At this point, we just wanted something fast and convenient. The day had been taxing for so many reasons, and more than anything we wanted to hit the hay and put it behind us, even though everything from the evening was imprinted permanently in our minds. It definitely didn't feel appropriate to have a nice night out on the town.

As we made our way down the street, a number of locals came up to us offering crafts, necklaces, pottery, and other wares. But after about 30 "no thank-yous," we were approached by a young boy with a big smile on his face, offering us a "good deal."

I don't know what it was about him. He was persistent, but he wasn't aggressive like the other merchants. Perhaps Stu and I stopped because of the kindness in the boy's eyes or the mere fact that his sales pitch was delivered with gusto and confidence. But for some reason, when he offered us his handmade bracelets, we both said yes. The bracelets were colorful and appealing to the eye, and they looked like they had been handcrafted with care. The boy told us they could be customized and fit to any size. Each bracelet was $3, but he would make us three for $5. We had no idea if he would even get them done in time because our plan was to eat quickly, get back to the hotel, and call it a night. But he promised that he would finish the bracelets for us while we had dinner.

Then he asked what letters we would like on the bracelets. To make it easy, we suggested "WTA" on all of them (which stood for World Teacher Aid, our initial name for the charity). At that point, Stu and I walked into a small café, ordered some pizza, and sat and watched the boy as he worked. He was amazingly efficient and clearly absorbed in what he was doing. There he sat working on the bracelets, wrapping and weaving string around some type of plastic, all on the side of the road.

We were intrigued by his process. Stu got up to go chat with the boy. After the ordeal of the accident we'd witnessed, I didn't feel like moving, but I watched with interest as Stu and the boy began having a lengthy conversation. A few minutes later, Stu waved for me to come outside. He was holding a piece of paper. As it turned out, the paper was the boy's report card, which was definitely a novelty. How many 13-year-olds do you know who carry their report cards around with them?

Stu asked me to take a closer look. He whispered in my ear, "Can you see if this report card is legit?" He presumed that because I was a teacher, I would somehow know if a report card from the opposite side of the world was legit!

So I looked at it closely. I could see the young man's marks, as well as his attendance record. He had gone to school 69 out of 75 days for that period. As we continued chatting with him, we asked if he liked school.

His eyes widened, and he said with the utmost sincerity, "I love school."

"Are you still going to school?" I queried.

The boy, who told us his name was King Willaim, said, "No." His shoulders dropped and his face fell as he explained that now it was his sister's turn to go to school. He went on to explain that his father had been hurt in a work accident, so it was up to him to earn money for their family. All of this made the accident that Stu and I had witnessed seem even more painful, as the reality that King William was describing hit close to home.

He went on to tell us that he earned money by making and selling bracelets to tourists. Some of those profits would go directly toward sending his younger siblings to school.

Stu and I looked at each other. We asked, "How much are your school fees?"

"About $40 a semester," he replied.

Right away, the wheels began turning; I could tell that Stu and I were thinking the same thought. We both believed deeply in the power of education, especially for young people who lived in parts of the world ravaged by war, conflict, and poverty. For King William, the difference between remaining stuck and having a future was a mere game-changing $40.

Just then, the waiter called. Our food had arrived. King William said that he would continue working on the bracelets and would have them completed by the time we finished dinner.

During dinner, Stu and I talked about possibly hiring King William to make additional bracelets in the future for our charity.

"Maybe we could sell them and raise some money?" I suggested.

Stu loved the idea. Almost right away, we also decided that we would pay King William's school fees. But we didn't want to just give him the money. There would need to be some stipulations in place, to instill responsibility and commitment on both sides of this partnership.

Once we finished eating and we paid our bill, we walked over to King William, who was patiently waiting at the curb. All three of the handmade bracelets were complete. As he handed them to us for inspection, he said, "That will be $5, please."

Stu and I shared our first smile of the evening. Deep down, I don't know if we somehow felt guilty about what had occurred earlier in the day. Maybe this was our way of trying to make things right somehow or to compensate for the roadblocks we'd met with at the refugee camp. Whatever the case, I absolutely knew that when bad things happen, the fastest way to turn things around is to give and make some goodness where you can.

So that's what we did.

Stu reached into his pocket and handed the $5 to King William. But then he said, "I also have something else for you."

William looked at us with caution and surprise. He could see that Stu had pulled out some more money.

Stu continued, "We have some more money for you, King William. This is for your school fees."

His eyes got very big, and his excitement was palpable. He looked at us with a mixture of disbelief and gratitude.

"But here's the deal," Stu explained. "You can't use this money for food, water, or anything else. You must use it for your school fees alone."

"Yes sir," King William replied enthusiastically.

"There's one more thing," Stu explained.

At that point, Stu looked at me and we both exchanged a conspiratorial smile. He turned back to King William and said, "If you maintain an A average on your next report card, and you send us a copy to verify you actually got the grades, we will pay your school fees for the next semester."

Never before had I seen a boy so excited for the opportunity to go to school. He lit up like a Christmas tree. "Thank you, thank you, thank you!" he gushed, as tears began rolling down his face. Stu and I also teared up, as we could see the purity of the gratitude and relief on King William's face. It was like we could see the burden he'd been carrying lift from his shoulders.

It had been a terribly emotional day for us, but we were so glad that the tears we were now shedding were tears of joy.

We parted ways that evening, not sure if we would ever hear from King William again. Although we exchanged contact information, we knew that the likelihood of staying in contact was slim. Still, we were hopeful that this could be the start of something special.

As we walked toward the hotel, we couldn't help but admire our hand-strung bracelets. They were beautiful, and we knew that if we could stay in touch with William, we could potentially sell a lot of them in our endeavors to raise money for the charity.

When we left for the airport it was with heavy hearts. The trip had not gone as planned, but meeting King William and seeing how passionate he was about furthering his education fueled a fire within us that had been dampened slightly by all we'd experienced in Ghana. I knew that meeting King William was some kind of sign—some kind of reminder of the importance of continuing to follow my passion for giving back.

It was about three months later, when I was teaching in my grade one classroom, that I got a phone call from Stu. At the recess bell, I made my way to the office to call him back. When he answered, there was no greeting, just an excited, "Babes, we got a huge package in the mail today. It's from Ghana. Can I open it?"

My heart started beating with anticipation. Could this package be from King William? In the months that had passed, we had thought about him often, but the hope of remaining in touch had waned somewhat.

Much to my joy and astonishment, the package was from King William. He had done it! Not only had he sent us the original report card that we had asked for, but he also added to the package a number of items that he had made. Included were sandals, more bracelets, bags, and even a tie with Stu's name on it. What made me smile is that within each thing he had made and lovingly wrapped in plastic, he'd included his e-mail address on a slip of paper. A true entrepreneur in the making.

In the current incarnation of our charity, Stu and I focus on making a collective impact as opposed to giving to individuals we meet. Still, meeting King William was a catalyst for all the wonderful things that were still ahead of us.

After our experience in Ghana, we recognized that championing someone and taking a stand for their education and well-being is about so much more than giving them a "handout." William was completely invested in his education, and the result of us believing in him helped him to take this responsibility very seriously. In many ways, helping King William felt like a case of joining our passion for giving back to his passion for pursuing an education.

Imagine the spark that you could ignite if you stood behind someone's passion and became an advocate for their higher calling. What can you do to give someone hope and change their direction for the better? Remember, you can make a monumental difference with as little as $40, a smile, a conversation, and genuine curiosity and care. As Stu and I discovered, a simple gesture can create a positive ripple effect that has the power to turn into a tsunami of hope, inspiration, and change.

PASSION NOTE

*What an amazing gift to be able to help
people, not just yourself.*

— BARACK OBAMA, FORMER PRESIDENT OF THE UNITED STATES

When you stand behind someone else's cause or mission and lend a helping ear or hand that moves them in the direction of passion, you help build a world in which people are looking out for one another's highest interests. You get to have the pleasure of being someone else's real-life angel, a gift that keeps on giving.

If you've ever been championed by someone who told you, "You can do it!" even when the going was tough, you know what I'm talking about. Someone else's belief in you can be the anchor you need when everything in your life feels hazy, uncertain, and tumultuous. At times it can be the one thing that gets you through. Wouldn't you love it if everyone could experience this?

A simple exchange and a mutual trust changed our lives and King William's life. Today, he is running his own business and even managing a small team. He still works with us and each year produces thousands of handmade bracelets, shipped right on time.

You might not realize it now, but you have the capacity to empower someone else to follow their passion, and to step into new possibilities. Think of someone in your life you'd like to support—it could be a promising young person you know, an elderly neighbor who's stepping into a new life phase, or the friendly barista at your neighborhood café who has a talent for making people laugh. It doesn't have to be someone you know well, but it has to be someone whose story and life stir something in you— that part of you that wants to see them shine.

Once you have that person in mind, write out a list of 10 simple actions you can take to support and champion them. Remember, this doesn't have to be about giving them money. Here are a few simple suggestions to help get you started:

- Write a few simple notes of encouragement for a friend, spouse, or child.

- Introduce or connect two people who you think can help each other.

- Offer to listen to a friend's new business pitch or idea.

Remember, every little gesture, especially when it's consistent, counts. So get out there and spread light and hope—the world is waiting for you!

Chapter 17

GIVE BACK
EVERY DAY

At this point, if you are someone who happens to be an introvert, or you have doubts about how your passion can make a difference and change people's lives for the better, I want to help you make the connection here.

If you haven't guessed already, I believe that the desire to serve and do good is pretty much hardwired into our DNA. The problem for most people is that they don't stop to think about how *they* can make the most difference. Hint: It's not by turning into Mother Teresa, unless you actually feel that's your thing. It's by embracing your passion, allowing it to move you toward bigger dreams, and using that passion as a tool to make the world a better place. Can you imagine what the world would be like if we all had this vision?

I know that I was able to dream even bigger when I moved beyond my individual self (and yes, that includes my ego and insecurities!) to think about the world around me.

We are all social animals who have the desire to contribute, but the thing is, so few of us realize that there are a million different ways to give back to the world. You don't have to write big checks or start global nonprofits. Your contribution can be as simple as a gesture of kindness or words of encouragement to someone who needs them.

Most of all, when we give from the place of our passion, we are connected to joy rather than obligation—which can make a big difference. For example, while I love being at big donor events where I get to share about Village Impact with people who want to step up and be a part of my vision for helping our community, I really enjoy traveling to Kenya and interacting directly with the people whose lives are being transformed. This is when I find myself in the zone, so to speak, because I am stepping into what naturally brings me joy and makes me feel the most alive—which in turn inspires me to make a bigger difference in the world.

Village Impact actually began years before we started it—when Stu and I began focusing on one of our shared buckets together, Giving. As Stu and I continued to refine our buckets, we simultaneously began searching for how we could implement kindness and giving back into our lives. This is still so important to us. Life is about making money to save, but it's also about spending your money and giving it away.

I remember making a large amount of money from something our first company had done, and while we banked some of it, we also gave some of the funds to a family member, who used it for a down payment on a home. This lit us up and was the start of what we now call our annual Super Surprise. Each year, my husband and I give someone an experience that they will never forget. Some of the bigger things we have done include paying for our family and friends to come to Kenya on our donor trips and taking friends to Fiji. Sometimes the gifts are anonymous, and sometimes people know they're from us.

I love having an impact in my community through random acts of kindness. For example, every Christmas we have something we call Give Back Time. This is when we spend the morning of Christmas Eve secretly giving to strangers—it's our family tradition. This can look like:

- Heading to our local coffee shop, where we give the person behind the counter $400 and secretly watch as they use it to pay for people's coffee.

- Taking quarters and taping them to candy machines.

- Hitting the grocery store and paying for the groceries of the person ahead of us in line.

- Going to a store and holding the door open for everyone who comes through.

- Dropping off unexpected cookies or treats to neighbors and friends.

When I'm onstage talking about Village Impact, I love discussing how it's the little acts of kindness that end up making a huge difference. On one occasion, a woman in the audience contacted me after my talk to tell me that she was on day 37 of a mission to sprinkle random acts of kindness throughout her day. I loved her ideas, which ranged from leaving a note of gratitude and appreciation for her mailman, to putting extra coins in people's parking meters.

What are some of your ideas for how to contribute your light to the world around you, whether that means starting with the people closest to you or even your neighborhood or town? Again, being of service can happen in so many different ways. The net effect of offering $5 to your favorite organization on a monthly basis, baking cookies for an elderly neighbor, or writing poetry for loved ones cannot and should not be underestimated. It isn't just the billionaire philanthropists who help create massive change; it's the everyday people who work to multiply joy by spreading their own.

An example is the concept of 100 Women/Men Who Care, founded by Karen Dunigan. Essentially, a group of 100 men or women get together and each donate $100 that goes to a local cause. They come together once a quarter to hear from three local charities who share their projects needing financial support. The group votes on the charity of their choice, and the $10,000 goes to them. So as you can see, one night, 100 people, $100 each, and $10,000 collectively can make a huge difference.

That's just one way, but think about it—when someone pays for your coffee at the drive-through, you get inspired to do that for the car behind you. And when someone offers a free guitar lesson through their business, it can get you to start thinking about the resources you already have that you can use to help someone you know.

PASSION NOTE

Kindness is a gift everyone can afford to give.

— UNKNOWN

How will you choose to give back and share your joy with others?

The ripple effect of a simple gesture is powerful. In fact, Stu and I share the fun with our entire family. Instilling the value (and fun!) of generosity into our children is deeply gratifying. Everyone, no matter how old they are, wants to know and feel that they are part of something bigger than themselves. They want to feel seen and heard. Generosity is a wonderful way of showing people you care and catalyzing the spirit of joyful service.

Making giving and generosity attainable and approachable is also something you can do for yourself. It doesn't matter where you live, how much money you make, or how old you are. Everyone can give.

Connect to your joy and curiosity in this very moment. What makes you come alive? Maybe it's playing soccer or arranging flowers. How can you funnel that passion into one simple gesture that will help another person feel seen, loved, and appreciated? I know that my passion for travel is woven into both my personal life and my business, and that it has also inspired me to give back to others by doing things like donating all-expenses-paid trips to people in my life. Whatever you come up with (and remember, it doesn't have to be massive), commit to doing it this week!

Chapter 18

HONE YOUR FOCUS

So now you know the power of daily acts of kindness and connection, which are integral to the impact you are going to make in this world. But you might be thinking, "Amy, I really want to do all those things, but I also want to make a difference by sharing my passion project with people. How am I going to do what I need to do in a way that has all those cool ripple effects you've talked about?"

As I mentioned in the beginning of this section, it's important to consider our lives in terms of both daily acts of kindness and a more long-term strategy for sharing what moves us with the world. One of the major lessons I've learned over the years about making a meaningful impact through your passion is that, in order for it to truly be sustainable and generative, you can't disperse your energy by doing lots and lots of things. You have to find that critical intersection between your gifts, what to focus on, and the right people to involve in your cause.

My friend Maria shared a great analogy for this, which she heard from author and entrepreneur Rachel Hollis at a recent event: It's better to take one soccer ball and kick it into the net than try to kick one ball a little way, then another ball a little way, and another until all three are in the net. Focus on what you want and are passionate about, kick *that* into the goal, and then come back for the others. You will make more progress this way.

Although Stu and I knew in our hearts that things would never work out in Ghana due to the many complications we faced on our trip, we had acquired some valuable lessons for the work that we still wanted to pursue in Africa—specifically, about what to do and what *not* to do!

After Ghana, we visited a school in Uganda, where we donated several books from our budding organization's Write to Give program (more about that later)—but the project itself was short-lived and primarily an opportunity for us to explore various models of doing the work we wanted to do. We felt that our contacts were still not complete, so after Uganda, we went back to the drawing board and asked for a contact in another country. This time, the organization we'd been working with (Global Volunteer Network, which had led us to El Salvador and the refugee camp in Ghana) gave us the name of a woman who has since been instrumental in our journey as a nonprofit. Her name is Irene Wairimu, although we like to call her the Mother Teresa of Kenya.

It was back in 2009 when we were introduced to Irene, who is the founder of Volunteer International Community Development Africa (VICDA). The summer after our trip to Ghana, we met at the House of Waine, a luxury hotel in Karen, which is a suburb on the outskirts of the bustling city of Nairobi. Irene was well dressed and animated, and she had a giant smile that immediately drew us in and made us feel at home. After Stu and I chatted with her about the work we longed to do, particularly my dream of building a school, she suggested a village a couple of hours outside the city that was in desperate need of a school. Although she seemed like a busy woman, she was happy to take us there herself.

Later that day, we jumped into her car and headed out. We passed zebras and baby baboons along the way, which was awe-inspiring, although to Irene, it was like seeing cats and dogs on the side of the road. We found ourselves in what appeared to be the middle of nowhere. There was nothing in sight but a few mud-constructed houses with blue tin roofs. These were the homes of families that had been forcibly displaced during the violent political election in 2008. Known as internally displaced people (IDPs), they had been relocated to this area.

Refugees in their own country, they'd been asked to build their own homes, which they'd only recently finished. The areas with these mud houses with the tin roofs were considered settled IDP camps, but there were also plenty of unsettled IDP camps across the nation where people were living in tents and even barns. Many of the unsettled camps were waiting for the government to send them to a settled area, so in such places—where the expectation was that people would be transient until they found a permanent home—schools were few and far between.

I wandered the site that morning; it had been raining, and the ground was wet. Threatening gray clouds loomed in the distance. I looked at Irene and asked, "How much would it cost to build a school?"

"It would be $125,000," she replied calmly.

Without even hesitating, I said, "Okay, let's do it."

Well, Irene was very surprised! She said, "I am more than willing to find another donor to help. If you would like, we could split the cost of that in half."

I shook my head no. I wanted to do it all. In my mind it was no problem that I literally had only $324 in my bank account. Did I know how we would do it? Of course not! But I knew that somehow my passion was being supported by the universe. And now I had a concrete goal: to raise $125,000. It felt scary, but somehow I knew that I'd met Irene for a reason. Being in this desolate area, in this settled IDP camp, I felt clearer than ever before. And I knew from firsthand experience that listening to my heart, to what I was feeling, was all I could do.

Remarkably, we raised the money to build our first school through simple word of mouth as we shared the difference we wanted to make with the people in our circle. We broke the cost down per classroom and asked within our community if anyone would like to donate and name a class for our first school. We sent e-mails and video messages telling our entrepreneurial friends about the community we had visited and our contact Irene. Miraculously, within a few months we had enough donors to build the entire school in the area where Irene had taken us. After the school was built, we invited those donors to come to Kenya with us, to experience their gift and get to know the community in which the school was built. What happened there blew my mind. Not only was our first donor trip a *huge* success, but every one of those donors who came on the trip donated again, which allowed us to complete a high school for the same community. And the fun part is, they came to Kenya with us a second time.

Another remarkable thing happened at this point. After more than a year of waiting, and after a lot of back and forth with the Canadian government, we were finally awarded charitable status!

⌒₭⌐

There is so much more to this story, but suffice to say we've built 14 schools in rural parts of Kenya, all with Irene's incredible and steadfast partnership. There was something about that meeting with Irene that cemented my gut feeling that this was it—Stu and I had found the place where we were meant to be. Perhaps it had to do with the obvious need for schools in Kenya's IDP camps, joined with our passion for education. It also certainly had to do with the feeling of ease and trust that we experienced when talking with Irene.

Aside from having started several of her own businesses, Irene heads one of the top women-owned exporting companies in Kenya—so naturally, her entrepreneurial spirit felt close to our hearts. In addition, she is someone who is constantly being recruited by government agencies because she is so highly respected in the communities in which she works. She has done a phenomenal amount of her own charitable work and is consistently asked to speak at international events. Given her formidable accomplishments, as well as her clear knowledge about her country's educational needs and her strong commitment to giving back, I knew that we'd finally found the missing link to turning this passion of ours into a sustainable purpose.

Overall, our journey helped us to recognize the importance of creating a system and process to keep our partnership thriving; but more than anything, it helped Stu and me to make progress toward identifying where our efforts would be best spent. We also recognized that in following our passion, we couldn't do any of it in a vacuum. We needed a trustworthy partner who believed in our endeavor as much as we did, especially since we were based in North America 95 percent of the time.

Like Stu and me, Irene has learned that fulfilling a sense of purpose is all about maintaining passion and remembering your *why*. Irene has shared with us, "One has to be focused and committed to achieve purpose in life. The accomplishment of purpose ends with a lot of joy. It has taught me that every day I wake is not about myself, but about others. It has taken me through a level of maturity where my priorities have changed. Helping people has become my top priority. There is nothing better in this world than positively impacting other people's lives."

Having Irene on our side helped us to hone our focus and decide on our ultimate mission: honoring the priceless value of education by building schools in rural areas of Kenya. Our decision was helped significantly by the fact that we now knew we had a trusted partner on the other side of the world who was in our corner and helping us to identify areas of greatest need.

Irene shares a strong connection to our vision, as well as our honoring of the ripple effects of planting small seeds, which is how we knew we'd found the right partner. In reflecting on her experience with Village Impact, she says, "It has made me think of how a small seedling of a plant grows into a tree that produces thousands of fruits over the years. When I look at the area of education, it all started very small with a donation of $300 per month to cater to an orphanage. Then—to a big pool where thousands of kids are accessing education every year. It has changed my beliefs—we only need to start a journey, and the rest of the world will join us. Any beautiful journey has a way of attracting masses."

With Irene's help, we have developed powerful systems and an on-the-ground team that directly connects with members of the community in which when a school is being built, all of whom are responsible in some way for the build—meaning they are deeply invested in the entire process, as is the government.

The government supplies the teachers and finances the everyday running of the school. In this way, we've ensured that our projects are sustainable, that the families in our targeted communities are actively involved, and that we aren't out there putting Band-Aids over all the problems we encounter. We're making long-term change, led by the communities that we have partnered with. By staying in our chosen lane, we've discovered that our capacity to make a meaningful impact is so much bigger than we could have imagined.

PASSION NOTE

All big things come from small beginnings.

— JAMES CLEAR, ENTREPRENEUR AND BESTSELLING AUTHOR
OF *ATOMIC HABITS*

You make a greater impact when you have all the things you need in place, and when you can begin to see the bigger picture of how your passion has the power to reach your desired communities. After meeting Irene, I could visualize what was possible in Kenya, from the very beginning to the very end (which was not at all the case in El Salvador, Ghana, or Uganda). In following the bread crumbs along the trail, and not giving up, Stu and I discovered that the stability and security afforded by the partnership with Irene would support the work we could do in Kenya.

Take a few moments to consider how you can hone your focus with your project, especially if it feels all over the place. Respond to the following questions:

1. What would I need to see this from beginning to end (e.g., reliable partnerships, a stronger mission statement for myself or my organization, etc.)?

2. What are the lessons I've learned so far (e.g., the audience that requires my help isn't the one I'd originally tried to reach, simple is better, etc.)?

3. What are the three things I'm most passionate about in this project?

4. What are the three things I know I excel at/do best?

5. How can I combine the last two questions?

Remember, the process of finding that sweet spot where you will gain more traction in your ability to make a difference through your passion will require trial and error. Stu and I are continually learning, changing, and growing with our charity and businesses—but the fact that we finally found our North Star in terms of a strong and impactful vision and mission gave us the focus we needed to change lives and communities for the better!

Chapter 19

KEEP YOUR "WHY" CLOSE TO YOUR HEART

One thing I've learned and that I tend to stress over and over to anyone who will listen is that making a meaningful impact that you can maintain requires that you also get to experience it. That's why I suggest staying close to the reason your passion was forged to begin with—by literally seeing, feeling, touching, hearing, tasting, and soaking it all up.

In order to be fueled by your passion project, you can't be consumed by stuff like administrative tasks such as fundraising and payroll. These things are absolutely vital, don't get me wrong, but I know that the closer you can be to the impact you are making on the ground—whether that looks like teaching painting to the elderly or making site visits to the populations being served by the organization you're pouring your volunteer work into—the more inspired you will feel, and the more likely you'll maintain the energy to keep going. In my case, I didn't even see the first two schools we built in Kenya until years later, as I was pregnant with Marla, and for a while, she was too young for me to take her. You can imagine how happy and reenergized I was to finally get back to Kenya!

I am forever grateful to the many donors who have been with us ever since that first fundraising call. Some of them continue to be our top donors, and some even sit on our board of directors. Our model has always focused on going deeper with a few key relationships versus trying to build surface connections with a whole lot of people. Like us, our donors have fallen in love with the work we are doing and have been an integral part of Village Impact's growth, which has been as much a part of their success as ours.

Why do I think this is so? Well, we have always emphasized that giving back isn't just about writing checks—it's about fully integrating and experiencing how our actions can impact others. And this cannot be done from a distance. When you are able to directly experience the impact you are making, it creates an unmistakable fire in your belly. Developing a personal involvement in whatever initiative you've chosen as your passion project helps you maintain a deep connection to whatever you're doing or what you're passionate about.

I go to Kenya at least twice a year to connect with our on-site team, as well as the communities that benefit from our work. There is truly nothing like it. Ever since building our first school, we've realized that the schools serve as so much more than places where kids get educated; in fact, they have become hubs for the entire surrounding community and havens where organizations and individuals from abroad can learn about the local culture and be inspired to offer their gifts. The schools are also meeting places for mothers, community members, and nonprofits from other areas (including abroad). A clinic is opening soon in the vicinity of one of our schools as a result of the stability that arose in the area after the school was built. The idea that we were a part of making that possible is incredibly humbling.

Remarkably, after Village Impact began its first housing project for our teachers, the Kenyan government decided to jump on board and build a home for the principal of that school. Overall, I get to see how schools are foundational in offering the surrounding communities a sense of hope, peace, stability, and possibility—and how they spark other organizations and even the government to make contributions to these communities.

∾

The stories that Stu and I share about our personal aha moments on the ground in Kenya also serve to spark something in the people we know. Once Stu was onstage at a live event put on by our friend, entrepreneur Jeff Walker. Stu became emotional as he shared that important epiphany he had about money when we were in Kenya, when he was speaking to the chairman of the very first community where we built a school. Stu asked the chairman how much it would cost to fund a full-time teacher; when the chairman said it would be $100 per month, that's when Stu made the connection that selling only one of his business's software licenses could support a teacher for an entire year.

"And then I thought, 'Well, what if I made a whole lot more money than just that one license? I could contribute even more!'" Stu shared, before turning to Jeff and saying, "You'll go to a whole new level in your business when you see and experience the impact that your generosity can have and is having. It has nothing to do with business in some ways, but nothing in my life has been more transformative from a business perspective."

Stu's story planted a seed for Jeff to come to Kenya with his wife, Mary, and see the very first school we'd built. This is something we always do when we take donors to Kenya: We show them the end result by taking them to the first school, so by the time we take them to the village where the school they are donating to is in the process of being built, they know what's possible. Jeff loved seeing the first school, but the roads we took on the journey to the community where the new school was being built were brutal. Jeff's school was literally in the middle of nowhere. At a certain point, the community met us on the road. Jeff just stood there as he looked over the ridge and into the valley where the new school was being built; tears streamed down his face in amazement. He turned to Stu and said, "Wow, I don't even know what to say." The principal-to-be gave Jeff a tour of the school, which was still in the process of being built; the entire meeting culminated in a beautiful celebration.

Since then, we've raised millions of dollars with the help of Jeff's Product Launch Formula community, since he has us on his stage every year. He has contributed so much to us individually, and because of his influence and passion for our work, he has led so many others to contribute, as well—something I'll be forever grateful for.

Our other online entrepreneur friends Amy Porterfield and James Wedmore have also donated money from their own pockets to help build schools in Kenya. At first, both Amy and James were reluctant to take the donor trip, as it can be challenging to move beyond the alarming headlines in international news. However, when we take people with us, they realize that what is happening on the ground is completely different from the stories that might circulate in the media and influence us. James went and absolutely loved it, and now Amy is preparing for her very first donor trip as I write this.

James has told us that although he went to Kenya with the intention to give back, he left with so much more. "Although it was easy to judge their current circumstances as poor (not even having shoes or clean clothes), I was overwhelmed by the gratitude, the kindness, and the happiness experienced by not just the children but all members of the community," he shares. "How can someone with so little and in such poor circumstances still be so happy? While kids in America get bored if a video game isn't challenging enough, these kids were playing soccer with a tied-up ball of old shoe soles. While we grew up dreading school, these kids walked miles barefoot just to come to class—and stay from sunup to sundown!"

For James, the experience offered an important reminder to always be grateful for what he has. And what made his involvement with Village Impact more extraordinary is that he had the opportunity to share his experiences in Kenya with his customers and audience. At just two events in 10 months, James and his community were able to raise more than $250,000 for Village Impact.

He explains, "Despite Africa being on the other side of the planet, our community saw the vision of Village Impact and gave from their hearts. To me, it's one thing to donate your time, effort, and money to make a greater impact in the world, but to be able to inspire others to do the same was powerful. Those who look up to us—as entrepreneurs, as leaders, as parents, and as role models—will model our actions and how we show up. When you realize that, you get present to just how much impact you have on every single person that crosses your path. And when you can inspire the people around you to give back, you aren't just making a greater impact—you're creating a movement."

Whenever we take donors to Kenya, we always hope that they will have the same experience that Stu and I did on our initial visits—and they almost always do. It is deeply validating to see the transformation that occurs in people like Jeff and James, and to witness how this firsthand experience serves to cement our relationships with our donors. Suddenly, giving back is no longer an isolated cause but something that penetrates the hearts and spirits of people who are stirred into action by our vision.

We see how our passion becomes wedded to their passion, and it is deeply gratifying. Again, it is about so much more than writing a check—it's ultimately about making the kind of heart-opening connections that truly reveal to us why the work we are doing matters so, so much.

PASSION NOTE

When you think about quitting, think about why you started.

— DENISE WALSH, ENTREPRENEUR AND SPEAKER

I always knew that the reason I wanted to join together my passions for giving back and traveling had to do with my desire to make direct contact with the people I longed to serve. I also knew that this transformation wasn't just a one-way transaction; that is, I have gained so much wisdom, insight, and knowledge about Kenyan culture from my trips to the communities we work with. I also get the opportunity to experience directly how what we are doing is changing the lives of our students and their families, and by association, their larger communities.

I want you to take a few minutes to write down a list of the main reasons *why* you are passionate about the project you've chosen to work with. (You might want to go back to the Seven Levels Deep exercise I mentioned in Chapter Five.) Here are some examples, based on my own experiences:

- Learning about other cultures and being transformed in the process

- Building confidence and self-esteem in young people, especially young women

- Spreading the value of generosity in a variety of communities

Now that you have that list, take a few minutes to write out a new list of specific actions you will take to stay connected to your specific whys. For example:

- Take at least two trips to Kenya every year and have meetings with the mothers in the communities we serve.

- Hire a counselor to connect with young women in the communities about the issues they are facing.

- Create videos that document our donors' experiences in Kenya, so that they can share the experience with their communities.

Sure, there will be times when you might have to burrow into responsibilities that take you further away from the very reason you are doing what you're doing to begin with—but please do whatever you can to directly touch into your why. Because not only will it change your life, it will also fill you up with the inspiration, energy, and motivation you need to keep passion your number-one compass in life.

Conclusion

Many people I've met who are inspired by the story of Village Impact and who long to dive into their own passion and purpose, in the same way Stu and I did, often hesitate. It can be overwhelming to decide where and how to spread your goodwill and intentions—especially if you feel that your life is a struggle and you're flooded with the many responsibilities of your day-to-day existence. But as I outlined in Part IV, it is so important that you keep moving forward to maintain motivation and momentum.

The key to making a true difference is not trying to take on the world, especially if you feel you can barely come up for air. Instead, take a deep breath and—you guessed it—come back to your passion. This is the starting point and the end point of making a meaningful impact, of living a life that in the greater scheme of things has been meaningful and fulfilling. You absolutely have everything you need to make that difference—you do—and it's not about having enough money or power to change the entire world with one grand gesture. It's really about fully standing in your integrity—in what moves *you*, calls to *you*, and fills you with joy and a deeper sense of connection to yourself and others.

I think about how Stu and I have chosen to live our lives in such a way that allows us to express our passion constantly and consistently. I think about how this has not only impacted the people who have received the fruits of our work directly, but also how it's touched those who have witnessed us in action.

We recently returned home from speaking at our friend Russell Brunson's event, Funnel Hacking Live, where we had the opportunity to speak and raise funds for Village Impact. While we were thrilled about the funds we raised, I could never have expected the call I got soon after. The call was from a gentleman named Barry Barbee, who sits on the board of the National Auto Body Council, an organization that gifts hundreds of vehicles per year to firefighters, EMTs, and other worthwhile causes. It turned out that Barry was in the audience at Funnel Hacking Live, heard our story, and wanted to help by gifting our charity two cars for our Kenyan team to use. This is SO incredible to us, as it's been on our Dream List. A car would give our team flexibility to get to a few of our more remote schools on a consistent basis when there are heavy rains and the motorcycles have no chance of getting there. Amazing.

This is the power of individual ripple effects. Our passion has the capacity to touch the parts of people that similarly yearn to do good in the world.

Today, Village Impact has raised millions of dollars, built 14 schools in Kenya, and educated thousands of kids. And through the ever-evolving journey (which, as you know, included its fair share of roadblocks and detours), we never lost sight of the impact we wished to make—both on a daily basis through acts of kindness, and through the development of a long-term strategy that would offer us all we needed to keep Village Impact going. This seamless weaving of our passion into the short and long term made such a huge difference—and I know that it will for you, too.

Let me offer you some encouragement that I believe will go a long way on your journey.

I want you to always keep in mind the deep impact you've had on at least one person's life. (And if you're not sure, please explicitly ask a loved one to tell you, because I bet you have made more mini-impacts than you realize!) Remember how it felt, and let yourself be uplifted by the fact that it doesn't matter whether you've helped transform the life of one person or a thousand people. The main thing is, *you did it*! And that's a sign of genuine power.

But I don't want you to stop there. Now think of how making that impact made you feel. Were you filled with joy? Motivation? A sense of determination that was bigger than your doubts or insecurities? Did it allow you to tap into the truth of the interconnectedness of all beings? Did it touch some core part of you that has an important role to play in humanity's story? Did it show you how you can allow your words and actions to align with your deeper intentions?

In truth, everything you do has an impact, whether you can feel it or not. You are learning to make your impact more intentional, and to let it arise from your purpose. Please don't underestimate how dramatically this can shift the world around you. Let it stir your heart and spirit. Hold it close. For not only will it fuel you—it will permanently transform you.

PART VI

BUILD YOUR COMMUNITY

If there is one thing Stu and I have learned over more than a decade of doing the work we love, it's that relationships are the bedrock of everything we are, and all that we strive to do—which is why I want to focus on what it means to build a community around your passion project.

Ever since our very first teleseminar fundraiser, we have recognized that living our purpose is all about creating deep and genuine relationships that promote unconditional love and support. In general, this is a philosophy we've always practiced, way before we even considered it a philosophy.

Especially because Village Impact has always been a small organization (with only eight team members when it comes down to it; that's three North American and five Kenyan ground reps and counselors), we've never had the bandwidth to do all the typical things that people who run a global nonprofit do when they are attempting to spread the word. But this has always been one of our strengths rather than a weakness. Despite the fact that we are a multimillion-dollar charity, you wouldn't necessarily know it merely by checking out our social media. As I've mentioned before, our preferred tactic has never been about reaching hundreds of thousands of people and getting them to donate—it has always been about nurturing a smaller set of relationships over the years rather than gaining a huge number of followers.

While the contemporary atmosphere around social media, entrepreneurship, and getting your message out into the world can unconsciously treat relationships in a transactional way (that is, "If you give me what I want, I'll be happy—and then I'll also give you what you want" or "This relationship is a means to an end"), it's important to have a much longer game in mind. Stu and I are not in relationships for the purpose of a single transaction, but because we know that true success comes from a collaborative effort in which everyone can benefit and have their needs met.

One of our early mentors, John Childers, taught us this valuable lesson years ago: In any relationship, it's imperative to ensure that the other party feels they got the better end of the deal. This is why we don't take any of our relationships—with donors, the communities we serve, the communities in which we fundraise, and beyond—for granted. The generosity that so many people have shown us is so humbling, and we don't want to forget any of it for a second.

So, our approach to building relationships is not about getting what we want and then moving on. It's about going deep with people over long periods of time. It's about sharing our passions with one another and cultivating communities in which kindness and connection are always practiced.

Our biggest donors today were friends of ours many years ago, and back then some of them weren't in a position to donate. Since then, a couple of them have launched businesses that rake in upward of $100 million, so now they are able to donate to us regularly. Of course, this wasn't anything that Stu and I ever predicted or expected, but it has proven to us that you never know who will be inspired by the work you do in the world, or how valuable the relationships you've taken time to build can be in the future.

In the same vein, we've discovered that cultivating a community from a foundation of passion has been revolutionary. Something magical happens when you connect with others by sharing your dreams. You begin to attract people who think like you, who are passionate in similar ways, and who have similar feelings about the world. These are the people who will help you make that light inside of you glow, and you will do the same for them. Working with other people is so powerful because it helps you to keep the dream within you alive, and to spread possibility wherever you go.

At the end of the day, as this section demonstrates, it is the passion and perseverance that you bring to your work that will rally other people around you. It is also the simple but often difficult act of continuing to show up and be an authentic friend to someone else that will create mutually beneficial relationships that are about so much more than what someone else can do for you.

Chapter 20

CREATE WIN-WIN RELATIONSHIPS

To build long-lasting relationships with people who care just as much about your passion as you do, you must first and foremost understand that you aren't asking people for a favor. You are providing them with a beautiful glimpse of the joy and purpose that are available to them through *your* vision. You are showing them what's possible and giving them a valuable opportunity to be part of a cause that will be just as meaningful to them.

In the beginning, when Stu and I started working on building schools in Kenya, we didn't talk about it to anyone. In many ways, we saw it as "the thing we do on the side," even though it was the center of our lives at this point. We also thought we'd be imposing our beliefs on other people by sharing our endeavors with them. We didn't want them to feel pressured to donate, and we certainly didn't want to guilt them into undertaking this huge humanitarian effort with us. So we stayed cool about it and really only discussed it when and if it happened to come up in conversation.

On our first donor trip to Kenya, our friend David Frey, who is on our board of directors, turned to Stu and asked, "Do you believe in what we're doing here?"

"Of course!" Stu said.

"Do you believe it's transformed you as a business owner?" David continued.

"Definitely," Stu replied. After all, our projects in Kenya had pretty much transformed the way Stu thought about making a profit.

"Do you think that if other entrepreneurs had the same experience, it would transform them?"

Stu thought about it. "Absolutely!"

"Then by not sharing the amazing work you're doing, you're holding back on sharing that gift with other entrepreneurs," David offered candidly.

Stu and I both had to sit with this reality and really let it sink in. Out of our fear of inconveniencing others, perhaps we were robbing them of the opportunity to connect with something that would literally transform their lives.

After that conversation with David, something changed in the way we approached our work. We were no longer as tentative about discussing what we were doing in Kenya, as well as the impact it had made on our lives, our businesses, and the people we were reaching.

And you know what? People loved it! They gravitated toward our stories and our passion. And they absolutely bought into our vision—to the extent that many of them wanted to be a part of it.

Most of us have the ambition to serve and help others, but many get lost in the vision and don't feel they have the practical knowledge to move forward. The amazing thing is, Stu and I were offering people an outlet to fulfill that ambition.

Sharing our passion with the world by talking about it more profusely gave us an opportunity to recognize that we weren't just trying to raise money; we were meeting a primal need in so many of the people in our lives. And we were deepening many of our existing relationships by strengthening the common bond of generosity. Nobody was doing us any favors, because inviting people to be part of our passion was a win-win!

One of the first people to share the win with us was David, who'd supported our giving-back efforts ever since our first tele-seminar for the El Salvador trip. He was a friend of Stu's, and he'd spoken at the very first event that Stu held back in 2006. David and I got to talking, and he shared with me his passion for helping people in developing countries. He'd always wanted to build schools in South America, and many years earlier, he'd been part of a missionary trip to Bolivia. He was a natural fit for Village Impact. When Stu and I were in the stages of officially creating our charity, we asked David to join our board of directors. He's since been on a number of donor trips with us and has helped us shape the direction of our organization in powerful ways. His contribution has been incredible and, in the process, he's been able to fulfill his dream of building schools in the developing world by being part of our work.

I feel so fortunate that we have similar stories about many of the people who have become board members, donors, and major supporters of Village Impact. Take our friend Michael Hyatt, who hosted Stu on the first stage we ever raised funds on. The event blew away all the previous events we'd been a part of, including the galas we'd hosted; in fact, after that one talk that Stu did on Michael's stage, we raised more than $60,000!

When Stu called me to break the news, I was so shocked that I began crying (and swearing, since I didn't know I was on speaker phone!). I was deeply humbled that in such a short period of time, we'd accomplished something we'd never done before. In fact, Michael is one of the people whom I credit with helping us establish our current fundraising model of speaking at large events and inspiring audiences with our story. For his part, Michael was so inspired by the generosity of the room that, the following year, he donated a portion of the fees he'd received from his popular mastermind. Then he built an entire school by himself, with a check he wrote to Village Impact in the amount of $125,000!

Michael was touched by the work we were doing because of his personal connection to Africa. Two of his grandchildren had been adopted from Uganda, and years earlier, he and his wife, Gail, had been to Ethiopia on a missionary trip. This was another clear case of a win-win situation.

And then there's the domino effect that we get to experience when we share our love for giving back on stages around North America. Our friend, entrepreneur and author Russell Brunson invited Stu to one of his mastermind talks to discuss our work with Village Impact; it was the first time that Stu spoke to the fact that people could donate to Village Impact by building a classroom. Knowing they could make such a direct and specific contribution really inspired people to want to know more. One of the mastermind participants, Scott Bradley, said, "I'm in!" That immediately led to Russell pitching in and donating a classroom, too, which led to our friend Bill Harrison joining us as well.

One of the major perks of donating a classroom or more to Village Impact is the opportunity to be part of our donor trips to Kenya, because as I mentioned before, this gives donors the rare opportunity to see how their generosity is making a difference. Many of our donors are also inspired to give their kids a direct glimpse into the power and value of giving back. Several of our friends have brought their spouses and kids with them on our donor trips, and every year that number increases.

Generosity is truly contagious. We love seeing mutual friends be inspired by one another's actions, and to experience the subsequent momentum. This is especially powerful in the context of live workshops and intimate masterminds, where we get to dive into our preferred method of relationship-building through direct connection and conversation.

And then there are the events we've been a part of, as well as the ones we put on through Stu's company and membership community. We absolutely know that we are meeting a need in our community by talking about our charity, because we are accustomed to fundraising between $150,000 to $340,000 at a single event!

None of this is about coming up with a gimmicky sales pitch, so I'm not going to give you any advice about that. It's all about bringing the best of what you have to the people in your life. It's about determining and understanding the mutual interests you share with your community and operating from the awareness that true service is about connecting with that community's why and offering them an opportunity to see it come to fruition.

This is a great way to build lasting relationships and triple your efforts to make a difference. Truly, everyone involved wins.

PASSION NOTE

You build a great network by first offering your services to others, and by so doing, winning their interest. This is the foundation of building trust and creating a platform for them to invest in you in a reciprocal manner, such that it becomes a win-win situation.

— OSCAR BIMPONG, AUTHOR OF *INSPIRATIONAL WISDOM FOR TODAY*

At this stage, you've found your passion, and your why—now you need to go and find people who will be enthusiastic about pitching in and helping you.

Yes, I want to encourage you to muster the courage to talk about your passion and to ask people to be a part of it.

Look at what you know and who you know. More often than not, when you share a clear vision with others, they'll want to help. In the beginning, the simpler your idea, the better. After that, the key is to write it down (in fact, I urge you to take an hour or so to do just that), e-mail it, say it from a stage, share it with a friend, but most of all get excited about what it is you're trying to do. And be sure to address how the work you are doing will also be beneficial to the people you are reaching out to. Try to put yourself in their shoes. And instead of touching on pain points, touch their passion points! How will their connection to your passion project fill their buckets and get their juices flowing?

If you feel hesitant about reaching out because you don't know where to start, or you don't feel you know the right people, that's totally okay. You may be like this woman in my mastermind who has expressed interest in wanting to collaborate with other people, but she isn't sure how to go about doing it. I will say that building relationships doesn't start by trying to be someone's best friend. It takes time, patience, perseverance, trust, and effort. Begin by talking with the people you know, establishing relationships with people who are doing similar work, or reaching out to those who could be allies in the work you are doing. This could be as simple as engaging with someone's content on their social media over a period of time and setting a respectful precedent for a future relationship.

Please remember that truly supportive relationships are ones where you're in it for the long haul. Ones where you want to enjoy meaningful conversations, experiences, and challenges together and mutually make a difference in the world. This isn't a quick fix or a one-sided transaction. It's about the multiplicative effect that occurs when people with shared values and passions put their heads together to create something beautiful in the world. So whatever you do, make your invitation from that place of deep connection, and people will respond!

Chapter 21

FIND THE RIGHT TEAM

Pursuing your passion is easiest when you enlist the right people to be on your team. This could mean hiring employees, finding volunteers, or selecting people to sit on your board of directors. It could also mean joining forces with people and organizations you trust.

Finding the right team is something any good leader values. If you've made it this far, you are absolutely a leader—and whether you have a global nonprofit or a passion for making the people in your neighborhood smile and laugh, spreading joy and generosity and a sense of purpose requires stepping decisively into your role as a leader.

This might ultimately mean hiring or recruiting the right people—the ones who will stand behind your passion 100 percent while complementing your gifts with their own. Finding people to help you can be hard, but amazing at the same time. It took me years to let go of the need to do everything myself, and when I look back on it, I wish I had done it sooner.

As you've probably heard before (and yes, I will say it multiple times, because it bears repeating), nobody does it alone—I mean *nobody*, even when it looks like a one-woman show. You can have greater impact moving forward as a team versus going at it solo.

I can imagine at least one of you saying, "I know I need help to get my passion out into the world, but I just don't have the capacity or time to build a team!"

I have great news for you: You can start small. One of my first hires was Carey Leader, who is still with me today. She came on as an assistant for Village Impact on an hourly project basis, until her hours slowly increased. As it became clear that I needed her business and organizational skills so that I could focus on fundraising, I eventually hired her as Village Impact's full-time operations manager. Today, this amazing woman runs the daily operations, makes trips to Kenya to connect with our five on-the-ground team members, and helps keep my life simple. Best of all? It makes the journey so much sweeter when you have people to work with, brainstorm with, and share your wins with.

I also love that Carey has progressively grown to take on a leadership role, to the extent that she has helped put systems and manuals in place for the daily activities of our team in Kenya. These days, I go to Kenya twice a year and also convene an annual staff retreat. I also take time to visit new communities in the area. Carey typically stays for five or six weeks after me and takes care of everything from paying site visits to the schools I am unable to see on my trips to filling out forms for our maintenance workers. Because she is on the ground for longer periods of time, she relays information to me that I wouldn't otherwise have access to, which makes me feel even more connected to my passion and mission. Carey's family grew up in Africa, so she has a strong sense of connection to the continent and its various cultures, which is a bonus.

The sense of trust I've developed with Carey has been tremendous, and it has also helped me become clearer about the tasks that I don't specifically enjoy and that I want to delegate to someone else. And, of course, because Carey's work with Village Impact grew over time, I didn't have to throw her into the deep end straightaway. I could allow myself time and space to build trust and slowly let go of the responsibilities that I no longer needed to hold on to. This also gave Carey time to learn the lay of the land and determine where she could focus her efforts. In fact, I think one of the reasons Carey is so invested in her role is that she essentially cocreated it.

And then there is the work we do on the ground in Kenya. Irene Wairimu was the very first person we partnered with, and she has five or six of her own staff members. When it was clear that we needed Village Impact employees who would help with the day-to-day activities across all our schools, I hired Chad McCordic, a good friend of my brother's, who then hired our first Kenyan representative at the schools—Sam Wangunyu. While Chad is no longer with us, Sam still leads our ground team in building community within our school villages. In addition, we have a team of therapists who address interpersonal and emotional issues within the schools and villages.

We also have a team of 15 builders, headed up by Irene's brother, Jackson, who has been with Village Impact since the very beginning. Funnily enough, when they began building our first school, we noticed that the process was moving along quite slowly. It turned out that they had purposely stalled on the project because they were afraid that when it ended, they wouldn't have another job. Needless to say, we've kept them very busy over the years. Jackson has also shared with us the ways in which he has grown during his time with us, and how he has been inspired by how the schools have contributed to ending the cycle of violence and poverty that so many villagers lived in, and how they have transformed the communities by bringing them hope.

I love heading to Kenya for our yearly staff retreats because I get to witness this transformation firsthand and to hear from our staff about what's working, as well as what isn't. All of us chat about our goals and how we can help each other meet them. The excitement in their eyes and their willingness to help on so many levels lights me up, and I know they feel the same way.

Getting to a point where I felt comfortable hiring staff and recruiting a good team was a long road for me. I had a number of fears and questions: How would I be able to sustain this decision, especially since our operational costs were low and the charity wasn't making a profit? What did it mean to now be responsible for another person's livelihood? Would I really be able to inspire my team members as a leader?

You might find yourself facing similar questions, but please don't be deterred by them. You will likely find that they mark an important turning point in helping you transform your passion into your purpose—just as I did.

We are so lucky that Stu's business partners, Andrew Ferraccioli and Asim Gilani, fully support the work we are doing with Village Impact—to the extent that the business has helped us fund a team by contributing to our administrative expenses. I am so grateful for this, because the act of hiring people changed the game for me. For so long, I'd treated Village Impact as a side project (even though it was my baby and my passion), and now I was being challenged to grow alongside my vision. My team was expanding, and it was clear that the charity was so much more than a hobby. It was my life's work.

In 2018, this helped me to finally let go of my teaching career for good—especially now that I had the help and support to let my passion lead me in greater and greater ways. While my husband and I do not draw a salary or pay for our work with the charity, I felt it was high time to devote myself to the cause and grow this passion into our family legacy.

PASSION NOTE

If you don't ask, the answer is always no.

—UNKNOWN

As your passion grows, the need to connect with people who can help you execute your goals in powerful ways will also grow. This might begin by enlisting the help of volunteers and interns, but it could also evolve into bringing on paid employees whom you trust and to whom you can delegate any of the responsibilities you don't want to handle. It could also mean identifying individuals and organizations who share your values, and who you know will help you take your passion from point A to point Z, and everywhere in between.

If you do feel you need to hire people, it's important to establish your priorities and your capacity to do so. Be smart about who comes on board. Are they creative when it comes to establishing systems and practices that will help you run things more efficiently? Are they just as passionate about your mission as you are? Are they good at communicating and working in a collaborative environment? Do you have clear role differentiation, so that you can both get your jobs done without any unnecessary confusion?

It's also okay to go slow, perhaps by hiring someone on a contract basis or for paid trial work. This will give you time to determine if they'd be a good fit for your passion project, as well as how they handle the workload and solve any problems that arise. I know some of my other entrepreneurial friends have sent out job postings with a challenge and have asked applicants to submit their answer to the challenge (for example, creating a new logo, a written report, or a short video). They then pick the best candidate from there. This is a great way to see a potential hire's skills in action before you even make the decision to hire.

This is a big step, so please take time determining your needs. Take a few minutes to write down a list of tasks that you could use help with. For example:

- Marketing and social media

- Website design

- Personal assistant tasks (scheduling, running errands, etc.)

- Sales

Now write down a list of the qualities that are important to you in the people you hire or work with. This might be a combination of qualities that are important to you in those you interact with, as well as qualities that are integral to performing the tasks at hand. For example:

- Flexibility

- Clear communication

- A great sense of humor

- Organizational skills

Now that you have a sense of what you want and need, practice writing a short job description for a role that is integral to helping you with your passion project. (It's totally okay if you don't actually plan on hiring someone; you're basically creating a profile for an ideal team member or partner in your passion project, which could also be a board member, volunteer, etc.) Maybe you need a public relations whiz, or someone who can handle all your social media. Feel free to create your description for a small project or a short hourly contract instead of a full-time job. Be clear about what you are committing to in terms of cost. Sometimes it's helpful to jump online to see if you can find any templates to follow, or even ask a friend who has hired before.

If you feel ready to take the leap, send the description to friends who can spread the word, or post it on a job listings site if applicable. Good luck in finding the team that will make your passion project sing!

Chapter 22

CONNECT WITH YOUR CHEERLEADERS

One of the most important and motivating aspects of following your passion is making connections with the kinds of people who will be in your corner all the way. This isn't about people offering you superficial flattery or agreeing with absolutely every decision you make—it's about unconditional support from those who truly stand behind your vision and want to see you succeed.

These are your true ride-or-die advocates, the ones who are rooting for you behind the scenes and giving you the advice and encouragement to keep going, especially when you are uncertain or a little burned out. These are the ones giving you real feedback, even when it's not positive. They challenge you and push you to levels you didn't think were possible.

Your biggest supporters might include mentors, family members, followers on social media, and people who share the same passions you do—basically, anyone who is there to nurture your growth and cheer you on as you follow your trajectory. They all offer support in their own unique ways and can be incredible allies who will continually remind you that what you are doing *matters*.

And let's face it—following your passion is definitely a personal journey, but we all need support and people in our lives who value our endeavors and want to see us succeed. That positive energy can do so much to lift our spirits and keep us focused and invigorated.

I couldn't write this book without sharing the story of Hay House CEO Reid Tracy.

Stu and I have both been blessed (and I know we are not the only ones!) to have Reid believe in us as well as our mission with Village Impact and our current business.

I had the pleasure of meeting Reid three years ago, as he's part of Jeff Walker's Plat Plus Mastermind, which Stu also participates in. (Can I say again that masterminds are a great place to find cheerleaders, as well as people whom you can also support?)

So about a year and a half prior to that meeting, I had the idea of renting a massive house on the ocean in California to host a private business retreat where Stu and I would raise funds for our charity—once again, mixing my love of travel with giving back. We had partnered with someone to help with the project, but unfortunately life threw some curveballs his way and he was unable to commit. I asked the owner of the house if he would give us a little more time to pull things together and recruit participants. That day, Stu had put an e-mail out to his mastermind group asking for ideas on how we could sell a business retreat.

A single e-mail from Reid changed the direction of our charity and our business.

It was one belief, one championing moment, one comment, one e-mail that—within minutes—helped us raise $100,000 for the charity.

Let me explain.

Reid suggested that Stu teach everything he knew about membership sites at our retreat and, in exchange, Reid would donate $100,000 to the charity and would also come to the retreat with three of his staff members.

Stu,

My offer is as follows.

I will pay for mansion for $10K and donate $100K to charity if you will teach us about membership sites.

I will also guarantee another $50K for 10 additional participants which I would offer to Plat first for $5K donation to charity, but will fill with my people if no one wants to attend from Plat.

Reid Tracy
CEO
Hay House

I remember Stu reading the e-mail to me as I was driving. I instantly pulled over the car and said, "Babes, you gotta do this!" I may have added some swear words for effect.

At that time, I had been encouraging Stu to share his knowledge and expertise about building successful membership sites with the world. For years, he had worked with entrepreneurs to help them build their businesses behind the scenes, but it was ultimately Reid's e-mail—and his generous offer—that gave Stu the final push to do it. Stu went from running the event with Reid to organizing three more workshops and building a huge community called TRIBE, with whom he shares all his incredible knowledge. It also gave Village Impact yet another massive boost in the world.

That experience was so memorable that every August 28, we send Reid an e-mail and video thank-you to mark the occasion. This is often done from Stu's live membership event, TRIBE Live, where he brings together more than 1,000 membership site owners. Reid will always have a special place in our hearts. He has been a major catalyst for our work in the world, because he gave us the confidence to build our charity and business.

Reid's generosity and investment in our success didn't end there. One of our major stumbling blocks as a charity was that the vast majority of our donors were American, which meant that we couldn't write them tax receipts for their donations—obviously, this was a significant deterrent for people who wanted to make larger donations and write them off on their tax returns. At first, we worked with an organization called Tides, which took a small percentage of any U.S. donation before giving the donor a tax receipt, then sending us the funds in Canadian dollars.

Then Reid came along and said, "I have a foundation. People can write their checks to the foundation, and I'll just turn the funds over to you, without a fee and in U.S. dollars." Amazingly, Reid didn't even want to take a cut. This beautiful gesture pretty much saved us and ensured that our faithful donors would have a good incentive to keep supporting us. It was also a win for us, as we send funds for our programs in U.S. dollars, which meant that we saved on the exchange!

〜

We all need our ride-or-die people—from mentors to that loving friend or family member who's always around to volunteer at our events or spread the word about the great work we are doing, with sincere enthusiasm. So often, incredible ideas and projects get stopped in their tracks, all because they didn't receive enough recognition, feedback, and support—all of which can provide you with the momentum and confidence to keep on keeping on.

This is why I encourage you to connect with people who inspire you, and who are mutually inspired by your passion and purpose in the world. It can be helpful to develop relationships with supportive mentors who've accomplished great things in a similar field, but more than anything, it's important to build connections that help you remember what's possible and that reflect the value of your passion back to you.

One of the best ways to deal with negativity in your life is to surround yourself with wise, positive people who will encourage you to grow, even if that means moving outside your comfort zone. Communities in which we all help each other thrive and shine tend to have a multiplicative effect, as I've mentioned before. So as you find the people who will encourage you to open bigger and better doors in your life, you will discover that you have the energy and motivation to do the same for others.

PASSION NOTE

It is important to have people believe in you. With this support, what you can achieve is limitless.

— RONNIE COLEMAN, PROFESSIONAL BODY BUILDER

I encourage you to take 15 minutes to have a heart-to-heart with someone who believes in you, and who has historically been one of your most highly respected and reliable supporters or mentors. A lot of people don't realize this, but the people who believe in you and your passion are the ones who are usually poised to give you the best and most honest feedback. We grow when we are able to take in not just the praise, but also constructive criticism that comes from a genuine and loving place.

Ask that person what they feel you are doing well, and what their highest vision is for you and your passion project. Then ask them what they believe you can improve on. This might include things like pouring more time into refining your marketing skills and public image, or changing the way you talk about your passion and share it with others.

It is so important to receive feedback from people you trust and whom you know are behind you 100 percent of the way! So please don't shy away from it. You definitely don't have to take all of it in, but you may discover pieces of advice that will be highly valuable when it comes to setting your sights on goals, projects, and possibilities that allow you to further expand your passion and impact your chosen audience.

Chapter 23

FORGE CONNECTIONS THAT REFLECT YOUR VALUES

I'm not going lie to you. Sometimes building a community requires setting clear boundaries around the behavior and values you stand for versus those which you don't. Creating a community that aligns with what is important to you is amazing, but it does mean there will probably be times you'll come up against conflict and frustration—and when you'll need to take the gloves off and be real and authentic with others.

This might not sound fun, but it is ultimately so rewarding to dive headfirst into hard conversations and deal with awkward or uncomfortable issues. I say this because I know that it has helped me clarify my values and be true to myself and my feelings. It also gives other people the opportunity to do the same, increasing respect, transparency, and camaraderie at the same time. As long as you take this as a critical opportunity to do better instead of taking it personally, the hard conversations can work wonders. They can also help you stop and reconsider what to do as a team to move the ship forward.

Stu and I have had plenty of moments when we've had to take off our gloves and stand firm. We've had those moments with communities we partner with, with the Kenyan government, with board members, with staff, with donors, with volunteers, with each other, and even with ourselves.

Yup, I've definitely needed to sit down and have a heart-to-heart with myself into the wee hours of the morning. Sometimes it was rough, but I made it through!

One moment in particular stands out to me, a moment when we had to be brutally honest with ourselves and a community with which we were considering a partnership. When the first school we'd ever built opened, I was nine months pregnant with my daughter, Marla, so I couldn't be there to celebrate the momentous occasion. Stu went to Kenya with David Frey, a board member, and a number of our donors, to participate in the school opening. Before the celebration, they visited another community with which we had been in extensive contact for some months about potentially building a school. As many of our donors on the trip were eager to support a new project in the coming year, it seemed a natural fit. On the day of the scheduled visit, torrential rain and muddy roads made it very difficult to get to the village. The vans got stuck in the mud, and Stu, David, and the other donors had to get out and hike almost two kilometers to their mountainous destination in the rain.

They finally arrived at the site—tired and dirty after pushing the van out of the mud, then getting stuck again, and walking in the rain. Even with all of that, they were excited to talk to the community about solidifying a partnership. But no one was present to greet them, much less discuss the possibility of bringing a school to the village. It was devastating and embarrassing for us as the leaders of our group. Here we were with donors eager to invest in this project and community and get to know the people who lived there, and it looked like there was no one on the other end of this partnership! Worse, they did not explain why no one was there and months of planning and resources were wasted.

The next day, at the official opening of the first school, the leader from that mountain community enthusiastically mentioned that he was excited Village Impact would soon be building a school in his village. Stu was dumbstruck, especially after the failed site visit. He looked him straight in the eye and said, "Nope, we aren't gonna do it. We planned that meeting for months, and you didn't show up. We can't invest hundreds of thousands of dollars in a community where the leadership doesn't show up."

It was a challenging and awkward moment, but Stu was resolute. And it represented a pivotal and fundamental operational decision for us. We knew that our partnerships had to be community-led. This meant that the community leaders we worked with needed to be fully on board as viable stewards of the project and, more importantly, as the drivers and agents of change in their own communities. This wasn't about us blindly dumping money and resources into any given village and doing all the work; we knew from our experience in Ghana that such an approach is flawed. Ghana taught us that community investment, beginning with consultation, planning and in-kind (local materials like sand and labor) and/or cash contributions were essential to ensuring ownership and commitment from the people who would benefit from projects. Since we build public, not private schools, this community ownership piece means communities are keen, engaged, and have the dignity of genuinely being equal partners. It also helps to ensure the sustainability of the assets provided and enables our projects to thrive for the long-term.

On that donor trip, we had our fair share of other uncomfortable moments that helped us refine and stand behind our values and the way we work with even greater conviction.

The Kenyan government, who also partnered in the project, predominantly ran the opening ceremony at the first school we built. Thousands of people had come out to partake in the event. The government gave our donors bread to offer the people in the village, but this well-meaning act of generosity quickly turned into a chaotic frenzy. Many of the villagers hadn't had a decent meal in a long time, and they were desperately grabbing for pieces of bread. It was distressing for everyone. Stu and I knew that we didn't want this to happen in the future. We were there to help deliver the priceless gift of education, not to exacerbate dismal conditions or place Band-Aids over huge systemic issues we had no business trying to address. However, the positive outcome was that this led to rich discussions about implementing breakfast programs in the schools that the community would run.

Then came the speeches. Unfortunately, Stu quickly realized that government officials were looking to use the opening of the school as a political platform to win the community over, essentially taking credit for the school build with no recognition whatsoever of our donors who had helped make it possible.

All of it left Stu with a very bad taste in his mouth. He was furious that the government was using this occasion to further its agenda. Later that day at an official luncheon, Stu found himself face-to-face with the national head of education. He wasn't intimidated by her rank; instead, he was honest and let her know we felt insulted that the donors who funded the building of the school and who had come all this way to celebrate the occasion hadn't so much as been mentioned.

It became clear through his exchange that she and the other officials believed the school was a one-time investment for us. They had experienced this many times before. Organizations would drop in, do a project that may or may not be sustainable (mostly not), then leave. Stu was able to communicate that we were in it for the long haul and that we expected to work as true and steadfast partners in community transformation. That conversation and standing up for what we believed earned us a great deal of respect and transformed our relationship with the Kenyan government. All the future celebrations involved our donors, and the government also took them as opportunities to give back by doing everything from donating school uniforms to planting trees to providing bags of grain to community members. It also seeded the positive relationships and lines of communication with the government that helps drive our success even today.

We've also needed to have hard conversations with donors about not offering people one-on-one gifts or donations. On that first trip, many of our donors brought items to give to community members. The problem is that gift-giving can create an unequal relationship and lead to an imbalance of expectations, ultimately disempowering them. It can often also create jealousy within communities and cause internal conflicts if some people receive gifts while others do not.

So, Stu and I had to get into that discomfort again and say, "We know you want to give away these extra items, and we commend you, but this is where you have to trust us and know that the long-term effect is negative rather than positive. We'd love for you to channel that generosity another way."

These days, we keep it simple by asking donors not to bring additional items; instead, as a group, we give out the same pencil cases or other school supplies to all our students in all the villages we serve. We want to be democratic and fair, and emphasize that we are there to offer solutions to the entire community, not to give gifts that serve only a few individuals.

These conversations have forced us to look carefully at what we are doing and why.

I'd love to say it's all rainbows and unicorns, but the daily reality of running a global charity has required making decisions and forging relationships that are in integrity with our vision. No matter what you are doing, I encourage you to do the same— even if that means having a few conversations that feel tricky or uncomfortable. Trust me, you'll be glad that you did.

PASSION NOTE

*It's not hard to make decisions once you know
what your values are.*

— ROY E. DISNEY, SENIOR EXECUTIVE FOR THE WALT DISNEY COMPANY

Take a few minutes to write down your primary values around your passion project. This will be your North Star that guides the relationships you build. I can't stress enough how vital it is to find partners who have the same values that you do when embarking on a passion project. This doesn't mean that you will always be on the same page, but it will create a level of trust, respect, and transparency that will help you move your work forward and make decisions that can be traced back to your overarching goals, values, and vision.

While you're at it, take a few minutes to write out some qualities that are important to you within each of the communities you are working with; this could include staff, board members, the people whom you are directly impacting via your message and work, etc. Some examples of qualities include:

- Responsiveness

- Honesty

- Reliability

- Humility

- An attitude of gratitude

- A collaborative mentality

And if you've never thought about this before, consider what is or isn't working in the current relationships that are involved in your passion project. Does anything need to change? It's okay if you end up determining that someone in your circle isn't quite the right fit, or if they are not embodying the values that are important to you. Take this as an opportunity to stand behind your values and to invite greater clarity and integrity from both yourself and the people who are helping you make your passion a beautiful reality.

Conclusion

In Part V, I shared how you can refine your goals to have an even stronger impact on the communities you reach, but if there is anything I hope you've taken from Part VI, it's that relationships move everything in the world. And no matter how much of an introvert you might be (hello, fellow introverts!), your passion project will come alive when it involves other people. None of us lives in a vacuum, and I'm going to bet that if you picked up this book, your passion project is absolutely invested in creating a better, more connected world.

So I encourage you to cultivate joyful, meaningful relationships that inspire engagement, excellence, enthusiasm, and deep connection. Trust your gut when it comes to whom you work with. Understand that having the hard conversations can create greater transparency, integrity, and connection with the people in your life. Know that it's not just about having people rally behind your project; it's also about planting seeds of inspiration so that they can connect to their passion and feel how it mobilizes them. And never underestimate the power of gratitude and humility. The stage management company that puts on Stu's and my events has told us, "We love your events, and one of the reasons we think people continue to come back is that you're so humble and so real." I hear this, and I don't ever want to change!

For us, building relationships isn't about putting on a show. It's about relating to one another at the most basic human level. It's about sharing stories, recognizing our commonalities, having meaningful conversations, and celebrating our differences. This kind of mutually respectful atmosphere will naturally gain you support. Stu and I have often been floored by how many people in our community have become unexpected advocates for our work, without our even having to ask them to take on that role!

For example, speaking expert and entrepreneur Pete Vargas had me speak at one of his events recently. He was a good friend who'd contributed by donating money to build a classroom, and he'd also brought his 11-year-old son, Keeton, on a donor trip to

Kenya. On the final day of Pete's event, he had both Keeton and me onstage. At a certain point, Pete turned to Keeton and said, "Aren't you excited that 80 percent of the audience have donated to Village Impact?"

Surprisingly, Keeton gazed out into the audience, and true to his 11-year-old honesty, said, "No, not really, because that means 20 percent of the people here haven't donated!" Keeton had been so impacted by his trip to Kenya that he really couldn't understand why the entire audience wasn't just as jazzed as he was. Keeton's impassioned sales pitch led to hundreds more people donating and then him deciding that his dad's event swag profits should be donated to Village Impact as well!

Just like Keeton and Pete, we've been fortunate to encounter so many individuals and organizations who've offered us their generous support—through donations, encouragement, or even just suggestions. All of them deserve credit for helping us grow and expand. And likewise, we've helped them plant the seeds for making their own impact in the world.

Of course, mobilizing so many people over the years requires effort. Sometimes we have to come out from behind our computers and actually call and talk to people. We have to make edgy requests. Sometimes, we must have radically honest conversations that make us a little uncomfortable.

This is where I want to emphasize that the flip side of giving is receiving, and the best relationships have a natural balance of give-and-take. Over the years, Stu and I have learned to recognize that generosity is incomplete if you don't know how to take in the goodness that is all around you. If you don't receive the bounty of what people wish to give you—in the form of money, time, facilities, etc.—you are depriving others of the crucial opportunity to contribute. So I hope you can begin to view your passion project as an opportunity to inspire generosity within your communities—and to build stronger, more supportive relationships in the process.

PART VII

LEAVE A LEGACY

The long-term vision for Village Impact is to grow and expand so eventually we can leave behind something strong and self-sustaining that all of the communities we serve—present and future—can continue to build.

What does it mean to leave behind a legacy?

I think of a legacy as a gift you generate with the intention that it be bestowed on future generations. Building a legacy isn't something to achieve in one fell swoop—and it doesn't mean having a monument in your likeness or your name on a building (as cool as those things sound). To me, it is the accumulation of all the acts of kindness and generosity that you have offered. To take it a step further, it isn't even purely about actions—it is about how you live your life. It is your principles, your character, and the difference that you made simply by being you and living in your highest values. I often think of legacy when I think of the poet Maya Angelou's words of wisdom: "I've learned that people will forget what you said, people will forget what you did, but people will never forget how you made them feel."

Your legacy will show up in a variety of areas in your life, not just your passion, but it's always most evident in the places where you direct your passion. Stu and I know that giving back isn't something that is limited to our work with Village Impact; it's hardwired into the way we live our lives, and the values we have chosen to pass on to our children. We want to live our lives in such a way that we inspire our children—as well as the kids who attend our schools—to pay it forward and to infuse their passion into everything they set out to do. We know that when we lead by example, we make the most powerful impact. And this is how incredible legacies get carried through the generations.

In understanding the legacy I want to leave behind, I realized that it's a lot less about one single generous act and more about developing a habit of embodying what I want to see in the world: generosity, patience, understanding, and confidence. All of these are values I want to pass on, and building schools in Kenya has offered me a vehicle to do that.

Legacy is at the heart of the work we do at Village Impact. For me, it wouldn't be enough to merely build schools where kids get educated. Our work is geared toward establishing communities in which kids break cycles of poverty and open their minds up to new worlds of opportunity. This is why we always stress the importance of entire communities coming along for the ride—because we are in it, and we want others to be in it, for the long haul. We want to offer individuals the valuable opportunity to provide for themselves, their families, and their communities, and to foster societies in which kindness and a possibility mind-set generate even more opportunities.

I also see how the legacy that Stu and I are building has impacted our donors. After a fundraising event, our friend James Wedmore told us that our story opened him up to a whole new world as an entrepreneur—one in which he could see how his work had the capacity to contribute more joy and goodness than he'd thought possible. I especially love it when our entrepreneur friends have this epiphany and share it with their communities, as it was such a big one for Stu and me!

Throughout this part of the book, I'll invite you to think further about your legacy and the long-term contribution you'd like to leave. I want to stress that this isn't about becoming world-famous or changing the lives of millions of people. Legacy is often quite subtle. And remember, it's ultimately about the person you want to be and, to paraphrase Maya Angelou, the feelings you inspire in others.

So take a moment to think about it, and maybe jot down a few notes. What are the values you'd like to instill in your children, as well as future generations? Which acts of kindness do you want to inspire long after you are gone? How would you like to be remembered? What positive attributes do you want people to associate with you? Most of all, how are you allowing your passion to be a foundation for the legacy you are building, right here and right now?

Chapter 24

EXPAND
THE VISION

A legacy is never set in stone, and as your passion flourishes in the world, your possibilities will expand accordingly. As Village Impact has grown, so has our capacity and our vision. As we have built new partnerships and interacted with new challenges, we've generated ideas that we might never have previously dreamed of. And this is great, because the through line is the same: the value of kindness and generosity that we want to inject into everything that has our name on it.

Currently, Stu and I are working on building an entrepreneurial program in Kenya for older students who've graduated from the primary and high schools we have built with Village Impact. Given our track record for building and maintaining so many schools across rural Kenya, the government agreed to partner with us on this exciting new project. The idea will merge our donor relationships with Irene's government contacts.

While we are still doing research to refine our ideas for projects and demonstrate the benefits that such an endeavor will have on the larger community, we believe in where our vision has taken us. Realistically, only some of the kids from our schools will go on to university, while others will need a useful and successful trade that will enable them to support their families and community and have economic staying power.

We were prompted to think creatively, beyond our model of giving kids a conventional education. While the idea for the entrepreneurial program wasn't even around two years ago, it arose organically from assessing our communities and getting a realistic read on what they needed that perhaps we weren't providing. This knowledge came out of discussions in teacher/principal meetings, as well as what we heard from the local community. We had to continually check our own blind spots and offer solutions that made sense. For example, some of our donors guessed what the community might need without being on the ground; a few suggested that we start a school to teach kids about computers and coding. But the reality in many of these places is that people have never even seen a computer before, and a few of our schools still don't have electricity.

Instead of introducing a bunch of newfangled ideas that might take several years to get off the ground, we wanted to be realistic about what the community needs and wants—which is why we chose to focus on entrepreneurial skills and self-development that will lead to them growing simple businesses that are relevant for their community.

I have always been insistent on protecting the values of Kenyan culture. We know that our Western way of looking at and doing things is not the only way. Stu and I know a lot about what it means to run a successful business, but we want to honor Kenyan social norms and ensure that the unique cultural experience remains intact. We've done our job as long as we've contributed to breaking the cycle of poverty and created sustainable opportunities that ultimately work to lift up the entire community.

PASSION NOTE

Vision without action is merely a dream. . .
Vision with action can change the world.

— JOEL A. BARKER, LECTURER AND AUTHOR OF *PARADIGMS*

How can you expand your vision? It's always a good idea to ensure that whatever you are doing in your passion project has a practical application and that you are forward-thinking and anticipating future trends in your chosen field. Take some time to answer the following questions:

- What do I think the field of my passion will look like in five years, based on current trends in technology, politics, economics, and culture? (If you don't know, it's a good idea to do some research or consult with other people in your field.)

- How might my vision need to change? (It's okay for it to change, by the way.)

- What are aspects of my vision that will remain consistent, no matter what?

- How can I ensure that I am able to keep my vision sustainable (since rapid growth can lead to burnout and collapse)?

- What are two to three ideas for possible future projects that will help me expand my vision and maintain relevance while also staying sustainable?

Chapter 25

INSPIRE OTHERS TO LEAD THE WAY

We've already talked about the power of creating win-win relationships with the people in your life, and I encourage you to do this every step of the way. In thinking about the legacy you want to leave behind, you can take this practice even further by motivating the people in your life to follow their passions and use them to spread generosity and kindness. After all, as a leader, your work doesn't stop at fulfilling your individual goals; it continues by inspiring members of your community to grab the torch and carry your vision into their lives, adding their own unique spark to the flame.

I want to take a moment to segue into a story about a powerful idea that began with planting modest seeds. As you know, when we were getting Village Impact off the ground, I was still teaching. I wanted to create a program in my school that demonstrated the incredible power of generosity and that would also raise funds for Village Impact, while at the same time aligning with the Ontario Language Curriculum. While I had participated in numerous hat days and candy days, I was searching for something that would be more meaningful in and beyond the classroom.

I ended up developing a program called Write to Give. In a nutshell, the program worked with five classrooms at a time, from kindergarten to grade six. One classroom would write the beginning of a story, creating the setting and the characters. For example, "Once upon a time, in the sleepy town of Waterford . . ." The next classroom would pose a problem. For example, maybe, "Charlie, the class bully, was not sharing with Kate." The third would pose a solution to that problem, the fourth the ending, and the final class would contribute illustrations. The books were then put together and sold on Amazon. What grandma, grandpa, aunt, uncle, dad, or mum wouldn't want to buy a book authored by a beloved child in their life?

The program covered expectations set out in the Canadian language curriculum, while the money raised from selling the books went directly to Village Impact. The community and parents loved the fact that it was opening their children's eyes to the larger world around them and that it was giving them the chance to think on a global scale. Incredibly, what began as a modest classroom project exploded into a global endeavor. In the early days, teachers would pass around their classroom's 100 words (as each section in the book was only 100 words long) in a Microsoft document, while Stu was madly designing the covers (and he's not a designer, so as you can imagine, things took a lot longer than they normally might!).

Over time, teams of classrooms around the world came together, and we improved our onboarding process with a membership area that included resources for the teachers and students. We also hired a legit designer, Chin Keller, who is still with me today. Over the course of a few years, I ended up overseeing the publication of 135 different books involving thousands of children from around the world, and you can still find those books on Amazon.

During this time, we also had Scholastic Education Canada jump on board to publish a book a year. We even hosted Write to Give days, where—with the help of generous donors, including a bus company that agreed to provide free transportation—we'd bring together the thousands of children who participated in the program to show them their books in the hands of Kenyan students through interactive presentations made by the Kenyan students featuring videos and pictures, as well as a presentation led by myself. During the day, we would celebrate giving back, Kenyan culture, and the fact that the kids were all published authors!

The process of bringing the books into fruition was deeply gratifying to the kids and teachers who were involved. Although the project grew and grew, it became clear that we needed to focus on other, more effective, ways to generate revenue for our charity and causes.

I've also been fortunate to be connected to people who've brought their incredible ideas into my organization. Ellyn Bader is one of the board members of Village Impact. She's a renowned therapist and is widely recognized as an expert in the field of couples therapy; she has also been at the helm of some innovative online training programs for therapists. Ellyn has been the primary person responsible for getting Village Impact's community counseling program off the ground.

Two years ago, we created a pilot project that would help children and their families deal with the violence and trauma they'd lived through during war and resettlement into the IDP camps, and to meaningfully address mental health within the community. This trauma had created unfortunate ripple effects in the communities, such as feelings of hopelessness, a rise in teenage pregnancy, and instances of physical and sexual abuse.

Ellyn brought a few highly respected psychologists—Sue Diamond, Peter Pearson Ph.D., Amy Crowe Ph.D., and Judith Anderson Ph.D.—along on a trip to Kenya, and they volunteered their time to train Kenyan counselors in implementing a culturally sensitive curriculum. She felt passionate about helming the program because she was aware that post-traumatic stress symptoms among refugee children are extremely high. The counselors now work in two different schools, and the transformation that the villages have seen is powerful.

⊂⊀⊃

There are so many ways to help people bring their passions and talents into the world in a way that spreads generosity, hope, and healing. One of the things Stu and I specifically love doing is inspiring entrepreneurs who have money to give. In effect, this is the true potential of entrepreneurship—it enables us to solve bigger and bigger problems, and to spur bigger and bigger change. Entrepreneurship is never just about the money; it's about what the money has the capacity to do, which is something our friend Russell Brunson knows well.

Russell and his wife, Collette, were both in it from the very beginning, as they were good friends of ours. Although he didn't have a direct connection to Kenya or children's education, Russell donated a classroom because he believed in what we were doing. He remembers the experience of watching a video that our board member, David, filmed outside the classroom that Russell donated: "It was 2011, and Collette and I hadn't been to Kenya yet. Then we saw these kids who said to the camera, 'Thank you, Russell! Thank you, Collette!' That was when I realized that we weren't just giving money somewhere—these were the actual kids we were helping. We knew right then and there that we needed to go to Kenya the following year."

Russell's business revolves around software he and his business partner, Todd Dickerson, created to help people build marketing funnels, which are automated systems that take a potential customer on a measurable journey through e-mails and offers for free content to becoming actual customers. Russell decided that for every customer who got a hundred people into their funnel, he would donate $1 to Village Impact. This immediately increased the amount of money he was donating to us, and it also took his community along for the ride, whether they realized it or not!

Russell has a quintessentially entrepreneurial spirit when it comes to how he looks at giving back: "When you're worrying about how to make your rent, you're limited. If you can set bigger goals, like figuring out how you can feed a hundred people, everything in your life gets solved—because you have to stretch further to meet that big goal, and it changes you. If you are constantly focused on yourself and how you can get yours, you struggle. But I've found that when entrepreneurs stop focusing on themselves and start focusing on how to best serve their audience, they have way more success—and then, suddenly, they are inspiring their audiences to serve their own communities, in turn."

Over the years, Russell has brought entrepreneurs in his FunnelHacker community to Kenya and has helped them recognize the power of giving back. Like us, Russell discovered that there is a big difference between giving money and giving time. "When you give your time, the level of investment is different. You care about people and a mission. I want to help entrepreneurs experience that," he shares. "My mission is to educate entrepreneurs and free them from what is holding them back, which might include being stuck in jobs they don't love. When you liberate and educate yourself first, you are in a place where you can help others. Witnessing Village Impact's mission gave us a way to help other entrepreneurs give at the next level— whether that's to their communities, family members, or kids who can't do it by themselves."

Russell has admitted that it took him a while to fully wrap his head around the mission of Village Impact. "The first year was very emotional. I was around all these kids who were hungry, and I felt so guilty as I was eating, knowing that they weren't. By the last day of that trip, I wondered: "Why are we wasting our money on schools? We should be feeding the kids!"

Russell remembers going to an orphanage in rural Kenya that had a breakfast program, and the despair and sadness that he felt, especially as Collette held a small baby who'd recently been dropped off on the orphanage's doorstep. After that, we took the donors to a different orphanage, run by a woman who was working to educate the children. "There was a different feeling here—one of hope and excitement," Russell says. "The kids were well dressed, and they were singing and happy. I remember realizing that the difference here was that Mary, the woman who ran the orphanage, was educating the kids. She was teaching them about agriculture and growing food. She was teaching them all they needed to know to produce resources for themselves, to be happy and have energy. That night when I got back to the camp, I realized I'd been wrong. Instead of feeding the kids for a day, we could give them an education so that they could eventually afford to feed themselves. I finally got what Village Impact was doing, and how the organization was working to make a long-term generational difference."

Now Russell and Collette go to Kenya frequently and have even built meaningful relationships with some of the students. They've had the privilege of returning to Kenya every year to see the transformation in the kids firsthand.

On one trip, they both expressed interest in helping other kids beyond the schools and communities that we serve. Irene put them in touch with a student who had dropped out of medical school because he couldn't afford it. Russell and Collette knew that the young man had the capacity to help his entire village if he graduated from medical school and became a doctor, so they decided to pay his school fees.

Years later, after he graduated, he took a 3.5-hour journey by motorcycle to the mountain where we had all camped out, to show Russell and Collette his graduation certificate and to share the tremendous impact that their generosity had on him and his community. The fact that the young man was now paying it forward deeply touched both Russell and Collette, as well as everyone else at the camp.

"We've had moments of being in the villages and feeling the hopelessness. But when a school is built and when these kids' lives are transformed, we create opportunities for more jobs, and for hope," Russell says. "And when there's hope, there's life."

It's so beautiful to see how our community members' hearts and minds open up and get even bigger, especially as they contribute their passion and insight. Through their work with Village Impact, we've seen so many people transform their businesses and communities, find deep personal fulfillment, and inspire generosity in others. Knowing that we have the ability to offer support to others on their own unique path of giving is one of the most positive and rewarding manifestations of the work we're doing.

PASSION NOTE

Remember that the happiest people are not those getting more, but those giving more.

— H. JACKSON BROWN, JR., BESTSELLING AUTHOR OF
LIFE'S LITTLE INSTRUCTION BOOK

It's so important to remember that your passion can be a springboard for someone else's. Take a moment to identify someone in your circle whom you can inspire to step even more decisively into their passion. Do they need encouragement? Advice? Is there an opportunity you can offer that will help them share their gifts and talents with the world?

I've talked to too many professionals who prefer to keep their knowledge to themselves because they view the people around them as competition. For me, success is about sharing and spreading the wealth, not hoarding it or treating our ideas and insights like proprietary pieces of information. There's plenty of love to go around.

Likewise, I encourage you to be generous with your time, energy, and encouragement. This is the meaning of true leadership. I love getting together with people in my community to share insight and advice about how to turn passion into purpose. Whenever you can, find opportunities to champion people in your life and to show them how their talents, passions, and actions can create meaningful change in the world.

Chapter 26

EMPOWER WOMEN AND GIRLS

In all the work I have done, I have always been deeply passionate about challenging gender norms that keep girls and women stuck in roles that limit them and prohibit them from using their passion to transform their lives and communities. I have worked with a number of women in my nonprofit and my business mastermind, and I have learned so much from them about what it means to overcome so many of the complex feelings we tend to experience when pursuing a life that we truly love and that we know will make a difference.

Some of the most brilliant women I meet struggle with uncertainty and guilt over following their dreams instead of laying it all down for their families. Thankfully, a lot of these brave souls have questioned some of this cultural conditioning and are proving to their daughters and future generations that it is possible to care for others while also tending to the garden of their passion. I've especially taken some pointers from the incredible women in the villages we serve in Kenya, who beautifully demonstrate that standing behind our passions and showing what is possible in a community can be a supportive group effort.

Wherever I go, I always try to be vocal about empowering young women. I love seeing my daughter, Marla, writing in her dream book about all the things she knows she is going to do, and the fact that her statements are "I will" statements, proving to me that she is a girl whose belief in herself will take her far.

Not long ago, I had a friend over for dinner and we went for a walk with the kids. During the walk, we passed by a beautiful home, and her daughter turned around and said, "I want to have a mansion one day." That's when my friend turned to her daughter and said, "You'll have to marry someone rich to live in a house like that." I paused for a moment, supressing my frustration with her outdated response, then gently suggested, "Well, maybe she will have a business one day and will be able to buy that mansion herself."

Many times we make comments to our kids and we don't realize that this is where the seeds of limitations begin. Simple statements like these can have the potential to shape a lifelong belief that ends up hurting rather than helping.

I strongly believe that as women, our words and actions matter. We lead by example, and if we use self-deprecating language or get stuck in the belief that we can't make our dreams come true, what is the example we are setting for our daughters? And even if we tell them that they can do and become anything they want to in the world, how will they believe us if we ourselves are living in a way that contradicts this?

Empowerment always begins with us, because our children are watching us closely, and they can tell when our words and actions are in conflict with our values. I am a strong advocate when it comes to helping women pursue their passion, because I have seen the cost of putting one's life on hold, and how this gets perpetuated from mother to daughter.

So if you're a mom, remember that you had an identity before becoming a mother. Therefore, motherhood is an "addition" to your identity, not a replacement for it. It may sound counterintuitive, but one of the most supportive and life-defining things you can do for your kids is to stay true to your passion and who you really are.

Think about it. Do you want your kids putting off doing what they love? If not, why is it okay for you to do so?

We really owe it to our children to live passionately, because they are impressionable human beings who pick up on all the things that remain unsaid. They know when we are acting from a place of genuine joy and vitality rather than mere obligation. They get a sense of what is possible by watching us live our own lives.

Recently, I wrote the following post on social media right before leaving home to speak at my friend entrepreneur Amy Porterfield's event. The post was preceded by the quote, "I want my kids to see what's possible for their life, by watching me live mine."

This was my bedtime conversation last night with my eight-year-old daughter:

As we snuggled and chatted about the week ahead she asked, "Mom, why do you have to go? Can't you just wait 10 years?"

Of course, it made me tear up a little as we chatted in the dark.

While I love sharing about the charity, I've noticed now more than ever, when I'm onstage the conversations revolve around not only the impact of the charity, but also my personal journey of overcoming self-doubt and fear around starting and running a business and charity.

As much as I love sharing, speaking terrifies me.

I do it, not only for the money we can raise and impact it will have on Kenyan lives.

But I also do it to show my children what's possible.

As I lay there in the dark, I honestly didn't know how to answer her question.

I'm heading out to California not only to speak, but also for my annual Lady Strength trip.

Seven ladies and I will be traveling down the coast in two RVs. It's always been my dream to mix travel, adventure, and giving into one, and this trip is definitely checking all those boxes.

As we snuggled some more, I responded with: "Marla, would it be fair for me to ask you not to do horseback riding for 10 years? It's important for Mom to follow her dreams and passions, just like you do. It's important for all of us to do this, no matter how old we are."

We snuggled some more and chatted about my trip, our next family trip, her brother, and the latest book she's reading.

> I had to smile to myself, because this little lady is a miniature me. She wants to know all the details, and she definitely has a passion for travel.
>
> While I know she's going to miss me, I think she also just wanted to jump in my suitcase!

The post resonated with women who follow me on Instagram and who also happened to be at Amy's event because, as women entrepreneurs, many of them also have full, family-driven lives. It made me so glad that I shared my experience, because I realized that beginning a conversation about something that isn't often shared or modeled in communities had the potential to generate a greater impact and perhaps also inspire women to have similar discussions with their daughters. Seriously, there's always a bigger net of people we can impact by being transparent about our passion in the world.

⌒#⌒

As women in the Western world, I know it can often be challenging in our compartmentalized, individualistic lives to get up and go with our passions. This is where I have borrowed some valuable lessons from the moms in Kenya, who follow a more tribal, village-based model that enables them to support one another and work harmoniously toward shared goals. In many of the villages where we've worked, Irene has helped women come together and form groups where each member gets the collective's financial support to start an income-generating project. When one of the women receives a loan from the others for the amount she needs, she pays them back when she makes a profit.

You can learn so much from the mothers in the communities, as well as how their passions directly impact the overall village. These are places in which caretaking doesn't rest on the shoulders of one or two individual women; all the women are devoted to raising up the community and their sisters.

I have incredible female friendships, but as a whole American society doesn't necessarily operate on such bonds of generosity and collaboration. I am in awe of how these Kenyan women balance the needs of the community with their individual endeavors as leaders and dreamers. It is truly inspiring. It is the kind of thing that I know has the power to inspire their daughters to be strong and confident, and to carry themselves with grace and pride.

I think of women like Norah Kiprono, a resident of the village of Lomolo A and the chairperson of a women's group that formed in 2015. It was Irene who initiated the project of empowering women by forming registered women's groups. Norah recalls, "Before, we used to stay in the dark, given that we only played the roles of housewives. Irene's initiative became an eye opener not only to the women in my group but to more than 200 women from the community who bought the idea of forming these groups."

The groups included training meetings where the women learned about group funding strategies, financial management, and how to start and operate small businesses. Norah says, "To date, we have really benefited as a group and also in our individual capacities as members. The greatest impact is that we have been able to get capital that is required for farming our farms. We can prepare our farms in time, buy seeds and fertilizers, and at the end of it all, we have food security in our families as we are able to put food on the table."

Over time, Norah and the other women recognized that this initiative rested on a powerful principle: "When you empower a woman, the family is empowered, the community is empowered—and this translates to empowering the whole country." How powerful is that?

I love watching these communities flourish in the capable hands of these incredible women, because it reminds me that creating a legacy of excellence and generosity is not merely an individual effort—as the old adage goes, it really does take a village, and it doesn't matter where you live. Everyone needs someone to support their vision.

It's so important to remember that turning your passion into a purpose is not a race or a competition. It is a collaborative effort that helps all of us express who we really are in the fullest ways we can. And it works best when we are all in it together and recognize that our individual fulfillment benefits our communities and creates vibrant relationships that make life worth living.

As the women in Kenya have shown me, we step into our full potential much more easily when we are supported and we see our highest qualities reflected in the eyes of our sisters.

PASSION NOTE

Every woman's success should be an inspiration to another.
We're strongest when we cheer each other on.

— SERENA WILLIAMS, PROFESSIONAL TENNIS PLAYER

If you want to be a force for change, I encourage you to support the women in your life to fully embrace their passions. Often, we become stuck in the mind-set that we need to figure everything out on our own, but the truth is, when we put our heads together we can approach our lives from a place of greater ease.

Take a moment to write down five simple ways you can support the women in your life to move in the direction of their passions. For example:

- Offer to babysit a girlfriend's kids so she can take that painting class on Thursday nights.

- Start a women's group or mastermind that helps women move their side businesses into a more prominent place.

- Show up for the women in your life—physically, mentally, and emotionally—when they are going through a rough patch and need empathy and support.

- Talk openly and transparently about topics like work, money, household chores, and how to create equity and balance in relationships so that women can feel less alone.

- Point out the talents and gifts of the women you know, beyond compliments like, "You look pretty," and encourage them to shine by pursuing what they are good at.

- Mentor young women in your life and offer them stories about how you got to where you are now, as well
  as moral support and encouragement.

Also, please don't be afraid to take up space by asking the
women in your life for specific support. Remember, relationships
are a give-and-take, and you need to fill up on your own fuel so
that you have the capacity to be generous with others. Practice
sharing your needs in a supportive community of women. We are
all in this together, and the more we are willing to be vulnerable
and ask for help and support, the more likely it is that we will col-
laboratively create societies in which our daughters will be one
another's most passionate advocates.

Conclusion

As you've made your way through the seven parts of this
book, I would like to ask you: Where are you going with your
passion? What's your longer-term vision?

So often, the question of one's legacy ends up being a question of strategy—and while there is absolutely nothing wrong
with creating a strategic plan for your passion project, I want you
to think about your long-term vision in a slightly different way.

I wish I could say that Village Impact has a replicable model,
but the truth is so much of what has emerged from this work is the
result of a whole lot of trial and error—as well as many consistent
steps (and stumbles) forward. It's about the everyday work we have
done to ensure that our activities and projects are aligned with
our values, and that we are exhibiting those values in pretty much
everything we are doing—from how we interact with our donors
to how we are engaging with the village communities in Kenya.

When it comes down to it, it's the regular ol' everyday stuff
that matters: the pleases and thank-yous and gestures of support
and acknowledgement. Who would've thought that all it takes
to leave a legacy is putting into practice all the stuff you learned
back in kindergarten?

Okay, on a more serious note, your legacy isn't something to ignore until later in your life. Remember, it's not made in a day or defined by a single action. It's about a lifetime of habits. It's about living in a way that honors yourself and the people in your life. It's about digging deep into your insecurities and doubts and forging ahead all the same. It's about becoming clear about what you stand for, and having the courage to put your entire passion behind that.

I think I'd go so far as to say that legacy isn't something you can just decide to leave—it has to be what you become. This means you are constantly working on and refining it.

Don't be daunted by the idea of your legacy. When it comes down to it, it's distilled in your daily activities, the communities you are a part of, the way you spend your time, and the way you show up for yourself and others. Ask yourself the following questions:

- What do I want to be known for?

- How do I want to show up in the world?

- What is it I love to do?

- How do I want to give back?

- Who are the people I'm deeply inspired by, and how can I carry the values they embody forward in my own life?

- What does all of this look like on a daily and monthly and annual basis?

The more tangible you make this picture, the easier it will be to back it up with meaningful actions, both big and small.

Live your life in a way that makes you genuinely proud. One of the primary ways you can do so is by living fully engaged, fully present, and fully passionate. Relish the teachable moments. Spread the wealth of your joy. Don't look back on your life with regrets or the sense that you were overly cautious. Go all out. You were born to do this!

AFTERWORD

You made it to the end! Congratulations!

I hope that this book has given you plenty of food for thought and filled you with powerful ideas for getting your passion project out into the world, or at the very least given you motivation to explore and revisit the things you love to do.

Of course, while you now have a general road map to follow, reading and absorbing all the information here is a preliminary step. When you put the book down, I encourage you to take the opportunity to act on all the knowledge you've gained so that you can put your important work out in the world. Find a community of people who will help you get things done and exercise accountability. Don't just let this book gather dust on a shelf—do something *right now* that will move you in the direction of turning your passion into your purpose. And if you're looking for a community of go-getting women who are ready to support you, I invite you to come and join us at AmyMcLaren.com.

I hope that it's clear to you that you don't need a brilliant idea. You don't even need to know what you're doing or exactly how you are going to get there. Your passion has a life of its own, and in many ways it's merely your job to get out of its way and allow your small actions to walk you toward your vision and create greater ripple effects in your life. I promise that the road will appear as you take more and more steps.

It's been more than 10 years since Stu and I started on this journey, and it is a constant adventure that has opened us up to the power of using our passions to give back in new ways. We had no idea what we were doing or where we were going in the beginning, but our belief in following our passions led to so many unexpected blessings, as well as support from extraordinary people. The fact that Village Impact evolved from a simple idea that continued to crystallize as we kept the faith and took action is humbling and allows us to maintain perspective and an attitude of gratitude every single day.

As you know, we have faced challenges and there have been difficult moments and choice points, which you will also likely encounter on your path. I remember the days when I was burning the candle at both ends and wondering if any of what I was doing was worth it. But I have come to peace with the ups and downs, and I realize that it is the daily work of showing up for myself and others that counts the most. It has brought me greater clarity and confidence about my vision, as well as a sense of pride that nothing can ever take from me.

At the end of the day, the thing that always brought me back to my passion and my values was my belief that, in life, we are meant to keep moving forward, not back. I knew that my deep desire to keep chasing the rainbow (even though there never really is an end) was the very thing that would fill me with the fire and aliveness that makes life truly worth living. Once I had a taste of what that looked like, I was not content to go back to the way things used to be. Catching even the smallest glimpse of how moving in the direction of my passion could positively impact so many others gave me the strength I needed to keep going. And there were so many little successes along the way that offered me additional fuel.

If you feel uncertain and hesitant about diving into the unknown, please know that you are not alone. Some of the most influential people on the planet have been in the same boat many, many times. I have learned over the years that this uncertainty can be taken as a blessing. When you are not attempting to follow a rigid path or be in complete control over your passion, you allow it to move with greater freedom and less restriction—and you discover tons of happy surprises along the way. New opportunities arise, and magic happens when you have the audacity to say yes to your passion.

When we share our story with people, we are always floored by the fact that it's not just the cause of our charity that moves people and stirs them into action; it's the story of our commitment to following our passion that gets them to think, "Maybe I can do something similar, too!"

If there's anything I hope I've conveyed in this book, it's that your courage and audacity to live passionately and purposefully have far-reaching effects. The world needs *you*. Just imagine the difference you could make in your family, your community of friends, your neighborhood, and your field of interest, if you devoted energy to your passion.

Take a moment now to consider the kind of life you want to live, based on the values that you hold dear. How can you tap into the talents and gifts that are your greatest treasure? How can you use those gifts to make an impact? What kind of world might you be helping to create? How many people around you do you think you would inspire? What would they go on to do, in turn? Now, in this moment, what's one small step you can take toward realizing your passion? Those small steps will lead to bigger and bigger opportunities, and your entire life will transform before your eyes.

The cycle of burnout that so many people associate with working hard to make our dreams a reality is an outdated model. Yes, your passion project will absolutely take work and dedication, but when you follow many of the principles I have outlined here, you will discover something that I find truly mind-blowing: The more energy you put into your passion, the more it will feed you—with motivation, ideas, allies and supporters, and so much more.

Your passion is like a magnetizing light that will draw to you exactly what you need so that you aren't operating from that excruciating place of figuring it all out on your own. While it has been obvious that my passion is travel, another thing I love to do is shop in offbeat places, scoping out the treasures. I love that as much as I love sweating in the hot yoga studio. All of this gives me energy and helps me appreciate my life and follow my main passions even more.

When you let your passion take the wheel in every possible way, there are no limits on the impact you can have and the people you can uplift and take along with you for the ride.

You have more power than you might imagine. The things that bring you joy *absolutely* matter, and they are the key to your greatness. Your greatness itself is a series of small actions that, when taken consistently, will lead you from doing something you are passionate about to expressing that passion as your most significant purpose and contribution in the world.

You don't have to completely transform your entire life. I want you to live a life that is more gratifying and passionate. I want you to get out there and use that passion to make this world a better place: for you, your family, and your community.

Say yes to the adventure that awaits.

With love,
Amy McLaren

ACKNOWLEDGMENTS

This book would not have been possible without so many people—it's hard to know where to start!

First and foremost, I have to thank my husband, Stu McLaren, for his constant encouragement and support through the entire process of creating this book. I love you so much and can't imagine my life without you by my side! You have inspired me since I met you. Most of all, I am thankful for you always encouraging me to pursue my dreams. The kids and I are lucky to have you in our lives.

Thank you to my parents, Nick Dow and Lynn Allan, who brought me into this world with a lot of love and encouragement to spread my wings and travel the world. You were the ones who planted the seeds of possibility and passion within me for exploring the world. Thank you for your encouragement and support from near and far. I will never forgot the trust you put in me for my first solo travel experience across the "pond," when I flew from Toronto to the U.K. at the age of 10. Thank you Ravindri Kulatunga and David Allan for your support.

Thank you to my in-laws, Phil and Georgie McLaren, for raising such a good man, someone I'm lucky enough to call my husband and best friend. Thank you for believing in Village Impact from the very early days of our classroom fundraisers and charity galas. You were always there to support us, and happy to help out.

Thank you to my brother, Jack Dow, and my sister in-law, Faye Ferraccioli, for also being a part of the charity since the beginning. You always were there to help when we needed it. Thank you to all of my family in Canada and the UK for supporting Village Impact.

When we started Village Impact, there were a lot of people, especially family and friends, who selflessly volunteered their time at our fundraisers, galas, penny drives, and more. Thank you for putting your hearts and souls behind our passion!

Thank you to the Grand Erie District School Board for always supporting the work of Village Impact, especially our Write to Give project. I'm so grateful to the two principals who gave me the opportunity to begin my teaching career, Kathy Ricker and Ron Code. Also, thank you to the Jarvis Public School community and staff; for several years, it was my home, and I am grateful to have had the opportunity to work with some amazing staff and parents in the community, especially in the early stages of building Village Impact.

I will always be grateful to our lawyer's office for that early conversation we had about the difference between a charity and foundation. Thank you so much to Mark Blumberg and your team of associates from Blumberg Segal, Toronto.

Thank you to our accountants from Gibb Widdis Chartered Accountants, Colleen Gibb, Elizabeth Mackin, and Kelly Roloson, who have been with us since the start, when our first year end was $300. Oh, how things have changed! Thank you to Nancy McKen and Leigh Sherry and his team from LJS & Associates for helping with our bookkeeping.

I am so grateful for my amazing staff and volunteers at Village Impact: Carey Leader, Elidah Wakanyi, Milkah Mwende, Philip James de Vries, Philip Muigah, Sam Wangunyu, Sylvia Brade, Euphemia Awuor, Maurice Juba, Brian Maode, and Julie Dulong. I love how our team has grown over the years. Thank you so much for the passion you pour into our work on a daily basis. Your work is changing lives every single day.

Thank you to Irene Wairimu, without you none of this would be possible. We greatly appreciate everything you have done to help our organization grow. Thank you to your staff and community at Volunteer International Development Africa.

Thank you to Dan Usher, Blake Goulah, Sam Mantini, and Dean Rainey for donating your time and making some of our first amazing Village Impact Videos.

Thank you to my husband Stu and his business partners at North Results, Andrew Ferraccioli and Asim Gilani, who cover a large majority of our administrative expenses, allowing donations to have a bigger impact in our communities. We couldn't do this without you. Thank you.

I am also so grateful for the team at Hay House. Huge thanks to Allison Janice, Tricia Breidenthal, Lindsay McGinty, Sierra Espinoza Figueroa, and Marlene Robinson. A very special thank you to Reid Tracy for his encouragement to write this book. A few years ago, I would've said, "That's a crazy idea!" And today, it's a crazy idea I'm so glad I listened to. Thank you for recognizing the power of my story, and for helping me share it with others.

I'd like to also extend a special thank-you to the folks at KN Literary Arts, especially my book midwife, Nirmala Nataraj. Thank you for putting your passion for words behind this project. I couldn't have done it without you.

Thank you to Bree Moss and Esther Nicula for helping create the first concept of the book cover. Thank you to Marlo Biasutti from M81 Creative for then taking the time to complete our first draft. Thank you to my friend Lindsey Mrav for making the cover as you see it today. Thank you to the photographer who captured the cover page and the family image on the book jacket, Erik Kruthoff.

Thank you so much to my always-supportive board of directors at Village Impact, many of whom have been with me since day one. Thank you to Braden Douglas, Collette Brunson, David Frey, Ellyn Bader, Carrie Woodward, Jeremy Laidlaw, and Nancy McKen! A shout-out to Ellyn for heading up and leading Village Impact's counseling program—and to all her therapist colleagues who stepped up to shape this incredible program: Sue Diamond, Peter Pearson, Amy Crowe, and Judith Anderson. And thank you to all of you who have volunteered your time to this initiative. I so appreciate you!

I also want to thank Braden Douglas's company, CREW Marketing, for the design of Village Impact's amazing new logo. Thanks for expressing our brand and work in such a clean and beautiful way.

I also truly appreciate the Kenyan government and the incredible communities in the villages in which we work: from the teachers to the students to the families to everyone else who has broadened that simple flash of inspiration while watching Oprah into a light that shines from one part of the world to the next. Words can't express how that makes me feel.

Also, a shout-out to all the personal development mentors, teachers, authors, and podcast creators—the ones I know and the ones I've yet to meet—for showing me what it means to stand in my values and believe in my dreams. I only hope that I can inspire my readers and community as much as you have inspired me.

Also, thank you to the many influencers and experts in the entrepreneurial community who have built entire schools by either having me and/or my husband, Stu, onstage to talk and share our vision for Village Impact or by conducting separate fundraisers within their communities. Schools were built because of these opportunities, and your generosity will continue to help thousands of children for decades to come. Thank you so much to Jeff Walker, Dean Graziosi, Rachel Miller, Reid Tracy, Ryan Levesque, Brendon Burchard, Amy Porterfield, Pete Vagas, James Wedmore, Michael Hyatt, Russell Brunson, and Todd Dickerson.

Thank you to the most amazing and talented event company team, Sage Event Management, and their founders, Bari and Blue Baumgardner, for all of your continued support while onstage and your attention to all the little details behind the stage.

I also want to thank those very first donors who came on our first donor trip and contributed to our very first school. Thank you Armand and Marianna Morrin, Russell and Collette Brunson, Jeff Dedrick, Ellyn Bader, Mark Jenney, Bill Harrison, Scott Brandley and Garrett Pierson. Thank you for trusting me. Thank you for letting me show you the magic of Kenya. Thank you for helping set the foundation for our current and future projects.

Words cannot express how thankful I am for all the generous donors who have fueled our projects. From the $1 donations all the way to the classroom donations and beyond, it all made a significant difference.

Thank you Kris Carr, Jennifer Allwood, and Kate Northrup for your support and encouragement.

Thank you to my LadyStrength community and mastermind for the ongoing support.

Thank you to Lindsey Hartz for her amazing leadership through the book launch process.

Thank you to Amy Crossley for helping design our promotional materials.

Thank you to Sheila Piesta, Leeiann Armonio and Helena Fernandez who have been behind the scenes helping our family since our children were little.

Thank you xo

ABOUT THE AUTHOR

Amy McLaren is the founder and hands-on CEO of Village Impact, a Canadian charity focused on delivering learning, leadership, and economic opportunities to conflict-affected children in rural Kenya. Passionate about inspiring and mentoring people to make a difference in the world, Amy leads adventure travel retreats and experience-focused events through her company, LadyStrength, helping women claim their passion and gain the clarity and confidence needed to live purpose-driven lives. She lives in Burlington, Ontario, with her husband, Stu, and their two children.

AmyMcLaren.com
VillageImpact.com

Hay House Titles of Related Interest

We hope you enjoyed this Hay House book. If you'd like to receive our online catalog featuring additional information on Hay House books and products, or if you'd like to find out more about the Hay Foundation, please contact:

Hay House, Inc., P.O. Box 5100, Carlsbad, CA 92018-5100
(760) 431-7695 or (800) 654-5126
(760) 431-6948 (fax) or (800) 650-5115 (fax)
www.hayhouse.com® • www.hayfoundation.org

⌒#⌒

Published in Australia by: Hay House Australia Pty. Ltd.,
18/36 Ralph St., Alexandria NSW 2015
Phone: 612-9669-4299 • *Fax:* 612-9669-4144
www.hayhouse.com.au

Published in the United Kingdom by: Hay House UK, Ltd.,
The Sixth Floor, Watson House, 54 Baker Street, London W1U 7BU
Phone: +44 (0)20 3927 7290 • *Fax:* +44 (0)20 3927 7291
www.hayhouse.co.uk

Published in India by: Hay House Publishers India,
Muskaan Complex, Plot No. 3, B-2, Vasant Kunj, New Delhi 110 070
Phone: 91-11-4176-1620 • *Fax:* 91-11-4176-1630
www.hayhouse.co.in

⌒#⌒

Access New Knowledge.
Anytime. Anywhere.

Learn and evolve at your own pace
with the world's leading experts.

www.hayhouseU.com